Overlooked

Questioning

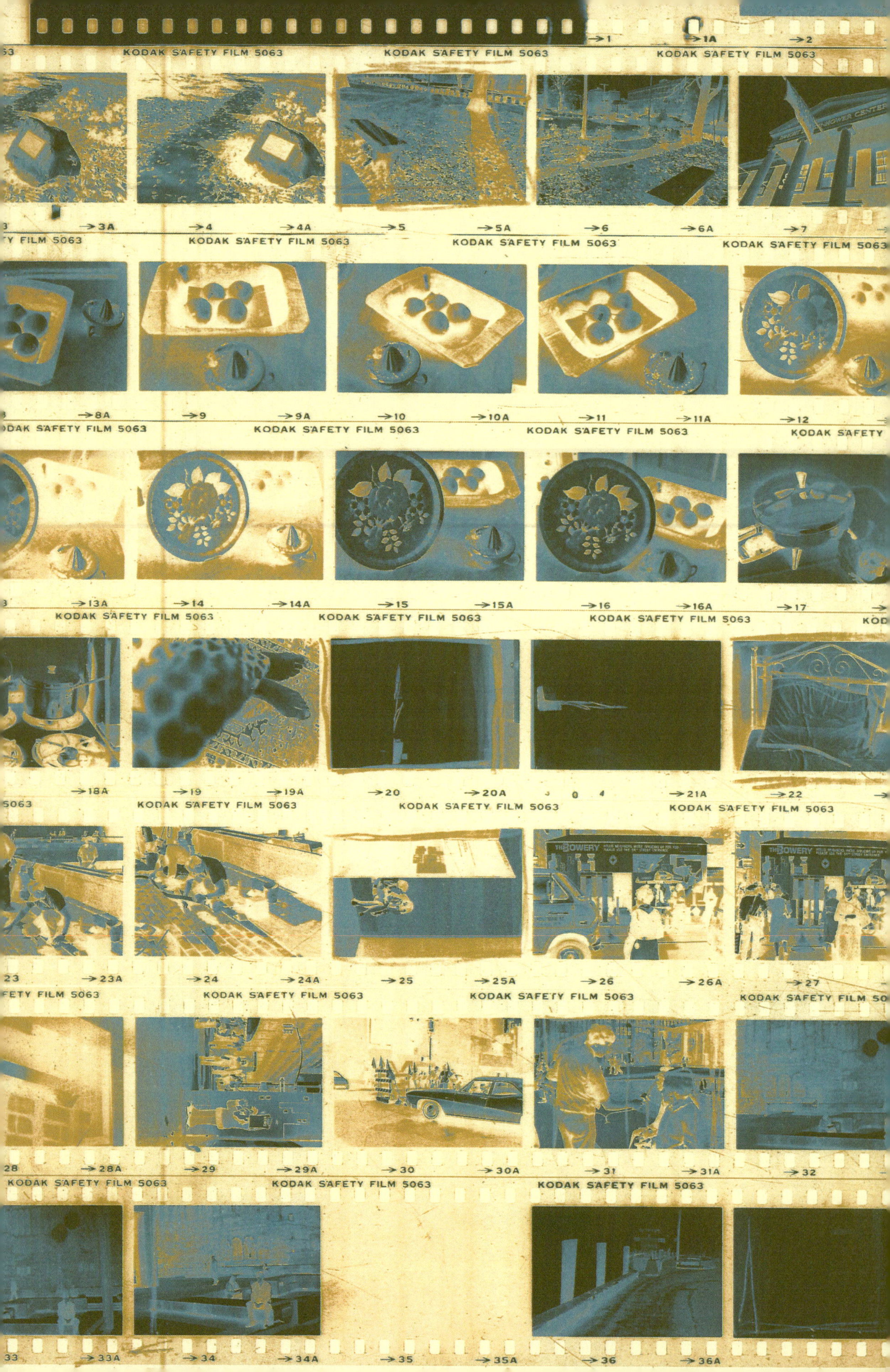
KODAK SAFETY FILM 5063

Note from the Editors

Is there anything as ephemeral, mundane, or difficult to capture as the everyday? For most, the everyday is not spectacular, provocative, or fiery. It may be easy to brush aside as unimportant or banal, especially as countless alerts of thrilling global events imply our own doings are mild and humble. For this iteration of LUNCH, we made a choice to dwell in this everyday space, look around a bit more carefully, and find the spectacular hiding in plain sight.

The everyday contains the quiet fabric of our lives, our routines, and the familiar places where we work, live, and study. The reliable infrastructures that tether our world together melt into the background, while the norms and practices that give shape to our social ecosystems may pass by unquestioned. Days blur together and become forgotten; days are spent waiting for the spectacular to save us from boredom.

But everyday is fragile. Moments of excitement, trauma, and displacement punctuate the continuum. What comes afterward is different. The river narrows and quickens, deepens and slows. The landscape of the everyday floods, inundating familiar landmarks and overwriting the ground itself, creating a new topography on which we rebuild. We mark the highwater line and carry on.

We've organized LUNCH 18 into four sections: Artifacts, Ritual, Overlooked, and Questioning. These arose from inherent tensions between our contributions, highlighting the richness and complexity of the everyday. Ritual focuses on the act of returning, while Artifacts reexamines that which is left behind. Overlooked inspects visibility and commonness. Questioning seeks to reframe our relationships to both physical space and ideas.

We hope this journal will provide you space for slowing down, shifting perspective, and finding beauty in the everyday.

Thank you for reading.

Sam, Margaret, Sophie, Michael, Sofia, and Ben

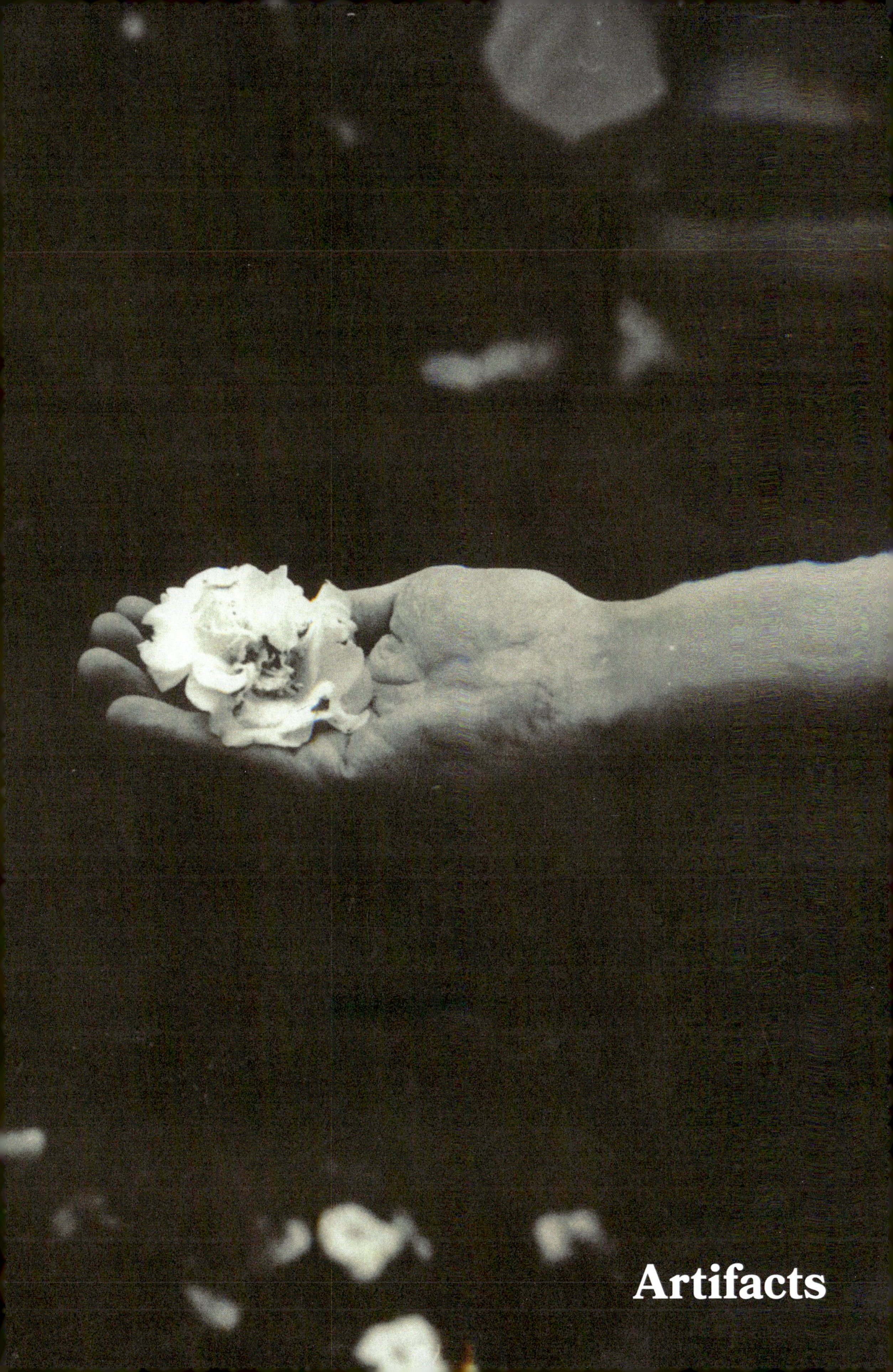
Artifacts

DAVIS

The Tenderness of Heavy Machinery

Isaac Cohen

As I travel through cities, I record great acts of tenderness masquerading as simple acts of security. A backhoe left out overnight reaches out and hugs a steam roller, offering comfort in the late hours of the day. It uses its arm to hold a friend tight and dissuade thieves. I see the bobcat and the digger sitting back-to-back, warding off the raiders of the night. I have taken to calling these efforts towards everyday security and care Machine Hugs. Heavy machinery in tender embrace.

What might be seen as a simple act of storage is a remarkable form of instrumentality. The machine does what it knows how to: it reaches out and grasps, it uses its size and weight, it pushes, and it pulls. The instrumentality of the machine and the ingenuity of the driver create small moments of personal connection in the midst of the chaotic urban environment. The last acts of a long day's work.

How do we value the everyday rituals of the individuals that construct our built environment? How do they store, care for, and secure the tools of their trade? The implements of craftspeople, how they make their living, are often the targets of theft. These crimes of opportunity leave people in the lurch, their livelihoods carted off. How are they defended against?

Hand tools may be taken home, but they can also be lofted stories above our heads, hung from the long chain of a crane.

Packed away and carefully secured, imagining their fear of heights at first, but relieved that they will be there in the morning to resume work.

What happens to the heavy machinery left on the street? What rituals are taken with the excavators, steam rollers, backhoes, and bobcats? This collection of snapshots represents the variety and ubiquitousness of Machine Hugs; from a dense downtown to a suburban high school the message is clear — everyone needs a hug after a long day's work, even the machines.

022402621
CB-224E

DEERE

About the Author

Isaac Cohen is an Assistant Professor of Landscape Architecture in the School of Architecture, Planning and Landscape Architecture at Auburn University. He has almost two decades of experience working on all aspects of urban park and public space issues. He has spent this time working with communities around the country on the design of varied public spaces, advocacy and fundraising to build parks, and on engagement and research into critical issues impacting the use of public space. He holds a Master of Landscape Architecture from UVA and most recently he was an Associate at Studio Outside Landscape Architecture in Dallas, TX where he brought a wealth of knowledge of Dallas neighborhoods, history, and landscapes to projects ranging from built works to city scale planning and equitable development efforts. His work has been awarded, published, and exhibited nationally and internationally.

Photos by: Isaac Cohen

Some Notes on Things

JT Bachman

Some things last a long time
Some things are fleeting
Some things we use over and over again
Some things we use only once
Some things we pass down to our children
Some things never get opened
Some things become clutter
Some things could really help someone else out
Some things get eaten by other things
Some things get buried underground
Some things float up into the air
Some things sink to the bottom of the sea
Some things stay
Some things go away
Some things don't ever come back
Some things have names
Some things are just things
Some things turn into other things
Some things remain the same
Some things can do many things
Some things do absolutely nothing
Some things are special
Some things are plain
Some things are tiny
Some things are very, very big
Some things are broken
Some things can be repaired
Some things cannot
Some things are too big to think about
Some things are hard to talk about
Some things make us laugh
Some things are kept secret
Some things are shared

Fig. A
Wasteland 01, 2023
Wood, Dirt, Polyurethane, Polystyrene

Fig. B
Wasteland 02, 2023
Concrete, Polyurethane, Polystyrene

Fig. C
Wasteland 03, 2023
Spray Paint, Polyurethane, Polystyrene

About the Author

JT Bachman is a registered architect, co-founder and principal of Office of Things, an architecture collaborative that explores the multiplicities of a constructed environment that is at once playful and rigorous, clean and dirty, high and low. Based out of in New York City, Chicago, and Charlottesville, OO-T's work spans a wide range of project types, including immersive architectural installations, interactive environments, retail projects, and strategic planning and design for contemporary offices. His current research explores methods of diverting material from landfill by reprocessing "waste" into new building material prototypes and/or long-lasting functional objects.

Bachman is an Assistant Professor of Architecture at the UVA School of Architecture. Prior to joining UVA, he received his Master of Architecture degree from Yale University, where he was awarded the AIA Henry Adams Certificate upon graduation. He completed his Bachelor of Design in Architecture at the University of Florida, and spent a semester abroad studying at the Vicenza Institute of Architecture. Prior to founding Office of Things, he worked at Studio Gang Architects in Chicago and the LAB at Rockwell Group in New York City.

FIG. 5.—Dolmen with cup-marked cap-stone, near Clynnog Fawr, Cærnarvonshire, Wales.

The Architecture of a Few Mundane Artifacts

Paul Mosley

Fig. A
Ritual Litter,
Sam Jacob Studio
(2022/23)

The late Italian architect and designer Andrea Branzi maintained a prolific career after his involvement with the radical architecture collective Archizoom. His writings and designs addressed ideas that grew more relevant over time even as they aged: the instability of program, ephemeral urbanism, and social change. In his book *Domestic Animals: The Neoprimitive Style*, Andrea Branzi prophesized that humanity was entering "a phase of strong reshuffling," a looming image of a "new normality" consisting of broader, deeper environmental and individual multitudes (Branzi and Branzi 1987). This uncanny intuition of what some deemed a 'new normal' came true following the Coronavirus pandemic, albeit not quite in the way Branzi imagined. Branzi's concept of "neoprimitivism" can be defined as a style of architecture and design that combines mundane things, advanced technology, and a return to nature. The synthesis of these three things in Branzi's work is evident as far back as Archizoom's 1969 scheme for No-Stop City. Its reappearance during this underexamined moment in the middle of Branzi's career is a parable that illustrates the promise of social actions, cultural imaginaries, and projected desires to attain a more expansive (and more cultural, less technical) relationship with nature. The roots of this approach is evident in No-Stop City's images of interiors showing primitive structures combined with electronic devices. As an approach to architectural design, Branzi's neoprimitivism can be read as an alternative to architecture's preoccupation with addressing ecological devastation through technological innovation.

The basis of No-Stop City is a familiar logic — essentially a synthesis of the traditional concepts of 'the city' and 'the countryside.' In his 2008 book *The Project of Autonomy*, Pier Vittorio Aureli traced the origin of this logic in No-Stop City to the *operaismo* movement in Italy and Claudio Greppi's critique of the 'city-territory' in the political journal *Quaderni Rossi* (Aureli 2008). In his diploma project at the School of Architecture in Florence, Greppi produced a provocation on the vast region of Piana di Firenze between Florence and Prato in which an expansive Territorial Factory erased the distinction between urban centers and territorial peripheries. Greppi's "Territorial Factory" appeared only one year before the formation of the Archizoom group and its isotropic logic, Aureli writes, was the impetus for No-Stop City, a theoretical model for urbanization where the grid becomes the seed for new formations of borderless urban space.

Fig. B
Digital Image © CNAC/MNAM, Dist. RMN-Grand Palais / Art Resource, NY

Andrea Branzi (1938-2023) architect. Dolmen 10 (2014). (left 3/4 view). Modeling clay, glass, wood, stones. 86 x 54 x 32 cm. inv no. AM2015-1-91(9) Photo: Philippe Migeat

This combinatory logic would carry into Branzi's work for Agronica in the early 1990s, a synthesis of agriculture and architecture, as well as his work with Nicoletta Branzi for the firm Zabro presented under the generic title Domestic Animals, a selection of his designs for furniture, clothes, and domestic settings produced between 1985 and 1986. In Domestic Animals, Branzi takes references from vernacular hybrids — primitive American garden gazebos, chairs made of oxen horns in Texas, among other references — and applies their authorless design languages to their own collection of designed objects. These objects are blunt yet avant-garde bricolages: natural elements such as sticks, logs, and branches are combined with more abstract architectural elements such as frames, planes, and posts. The catalog for Domestic Animals contains tables, chairs, shelving, wardrobes, and other furniture pieces that absorb this logic, showing abstract architectural shapes with striped rods symbolizing 'natural' elements, mostly the legs of furniture. As fabricated objects, these legs become segments from birch tree branches and sections of tree trunks with the bark still attached, among other natural elements. These bricolages speak to both architecture and nature for what they are: artificial constructs (Branzi and Branzi 1987).

The strangely current yet prehistoric tone of Domestic Animals resonates with the work of some discursive contemporary architecture and design practices including Sam Jacob Studio (SJS), First Office, Anne Holtrop, and Ensamble Studio, among others. For example, SJS's "Summer Awakening," designed for Selfridges London in 2021, consists of three installations that combine neolithic objects with modern geometric forms. In one of these installations, a massive stone in the shape of a wheel rests on a tilted triangular prism like a wheel stop. In another, groups of spindly precarious

ANDREA BRANZI 2014

columns hold stacks of stone-like slabs, crowned with the silhouette of a neon sun. Each of the three installations represent the phases of a summer's day: dawn, noon, and dusk. Their 2022-23 exhibition "Against Nature" highlights this hybrid logic, where abstract primary shapes are collaged into the naturalistic, representational scenes of second-hand paintings and etchings. Their 2022 Yantian Dolmen (a dolmen is a type of megalith consisting of large upright stones supporting a horizontal capstone, like a table) mixes elements of everyday municipal street furniture with objects that appear ancient. Given the striped furniture legs in the catalog for Domestic Animals, one can speculate that the precarious striped columns of this urban dolmen is a reference to Branzi. First Office's PS1 Dolmen is another example. Around 2014, Branzi himself was experimenting with Dolmens. The neoprimitive dimension of this work is far from Luddite musings on environmentalism and globalization. On the contrary, many of these projects use advanced technology. Both SJS and Ensamble Studio have used photogrammetry technology to replicate the complex textures and features of stone. Ensamble's 2018 project for Ca'n Terra in Menorca, Spain — a "house of the earth" — is one example. This project retrofits a former stone quarry into a domestic environment using scanning technology with millimetric precision. Their neolithic references suggest new forms of ritual use and symbolic function as a critique of technology even as it embraces technology. Yet this work surpasses the pitfalls of subjective interpretation and symbolism by engaging with the idea of 'primitivism' within our hypermediated and global field of architecture. In *Scorched Earth* critic Jonathan Crary observes that "the internet overwhelming[ly]

Fig. C
Yantian Dolmen, Yantian port district, Shenzhen, Sam Jacob Studio (2020)

Fig. D
Summer Awakening, London, UK, Sam Jacob Studio (2021)

produces self-interested subjectivities incapable of imagining goals or outcomes other than private, individual ones." (Crary 2022). These new forms of primitivism in architecture, as well as new archeological discoveries in anthropology may be the answer to Crary's critique of digital technology.

The anthropological dimension of these architectural practices resonate with new scholarship on neolithic archaeology. David Graeber and David Wengrow, in *The Dawn of Everything*, observe that Neolithic ecology wasn't about squeezing as many calories out of the earth as possible, as with contemporary agriculture. Rather, they ask: "What if we shifted the emphasis away from agriculture and domestication to, say, botany or even gardening ?" Neolithic botanists were more concerned, "with creating garden plots — artificial, often temporary habitats — in which the ecological scales were tipped in favour of preferred species. Their 'laboratory' was the real world of plants and animals, whose innate tendencies they exploited through close experimentation" (Graeber and Wengrow 2021). This quote suggests that our neolithic ancestors maintained a balanced relationship with ecosystems through sustainable land management practices — a deliberate practice that Graeber and Wengrow call "neolithic science." This primitive science, before the formation of the sciences, reveals an intelligent approach to land alteration where both humans and other life forms benefit. Graeber and Wengrow provide archeological evidence that early humans applied this 'neolithic science' to sustainable land management practices for thousands of years, thereby extending, building, and enhancing natural habitats, revealing that for large expanses of human history an ecological balance was maintained between natural habitats and anthropogenic manipulations of those habitats (Graeber and Wengrow 2021). And this is the promise of neoprimitivism: if the term can be used to describe a tendency in contemporary architecture and design, then the laboratory for experimentation in this work is the 'real world' of ecosystems, natural habitat, and biomes — areas of nature under threat of loss and disappearance.

What if Branzi's logic of synthesis were applied to the symbiotic approach of neolithic botanists? A possible answer to this question might involve revisioning No-Stop City not as a theoretical model for urbanizing the countryside or ruralizing the city, but rather as a model for urbanization that accommodates the restoration and expansion of ecosystems, biomes, and natural areas. Common to the work of the contemporary designers discussed in this essay, Graeber and Wengrow's observations on "neolithic science," and Branzi's mundane artifacts is a reflection on the underdiscussed tendency of primitivism in contemporary architecture and its strong ecological potential.

Fig. E
Summer Awakening, London, UK, Sam Jacob Studio (2021)

References:

Aureli, Pier Vittorio. *The Project of Autonomy: Politics and Architecture within and against Capitalism*. Princeton, NJ: Princeton Architectural Press, 2008.

Branzi, Andrea and Nicoletta Branzi. *Domestic Animals: The Neoprimitive Style*. Cambridge, MA: MIT Press, 1987.

Crary, Jonathan. *Scorched Earth: Beyond the Digital Age to a Post-Capitalist World*. New York and London: Verso, 2022.

Graeber, David and David Wengrow. *The Dawn of Everything: A New History of Humanity*. New York: Farrar, Straus and Giroux, 2021.

About the Author

Paul Mosley is an Assistant Professor of Architecture and Urban Design at Kent State University. His creative activity, writing, and teaching focuses on renewing architecture's urban relevance as a catalyst for environmental restoration. He previously worked at Marlon Blackwell Architects, SOM in Chicago, and Log Journal. He holds an MSArch and MA in Design Criticism from the UIC School of Architecture, and a BArch from the Fay Jones School of Architecture. His writing has appeared in Architect's Newspaper, Drawing Matter, and Log among other publications.

ROLEX

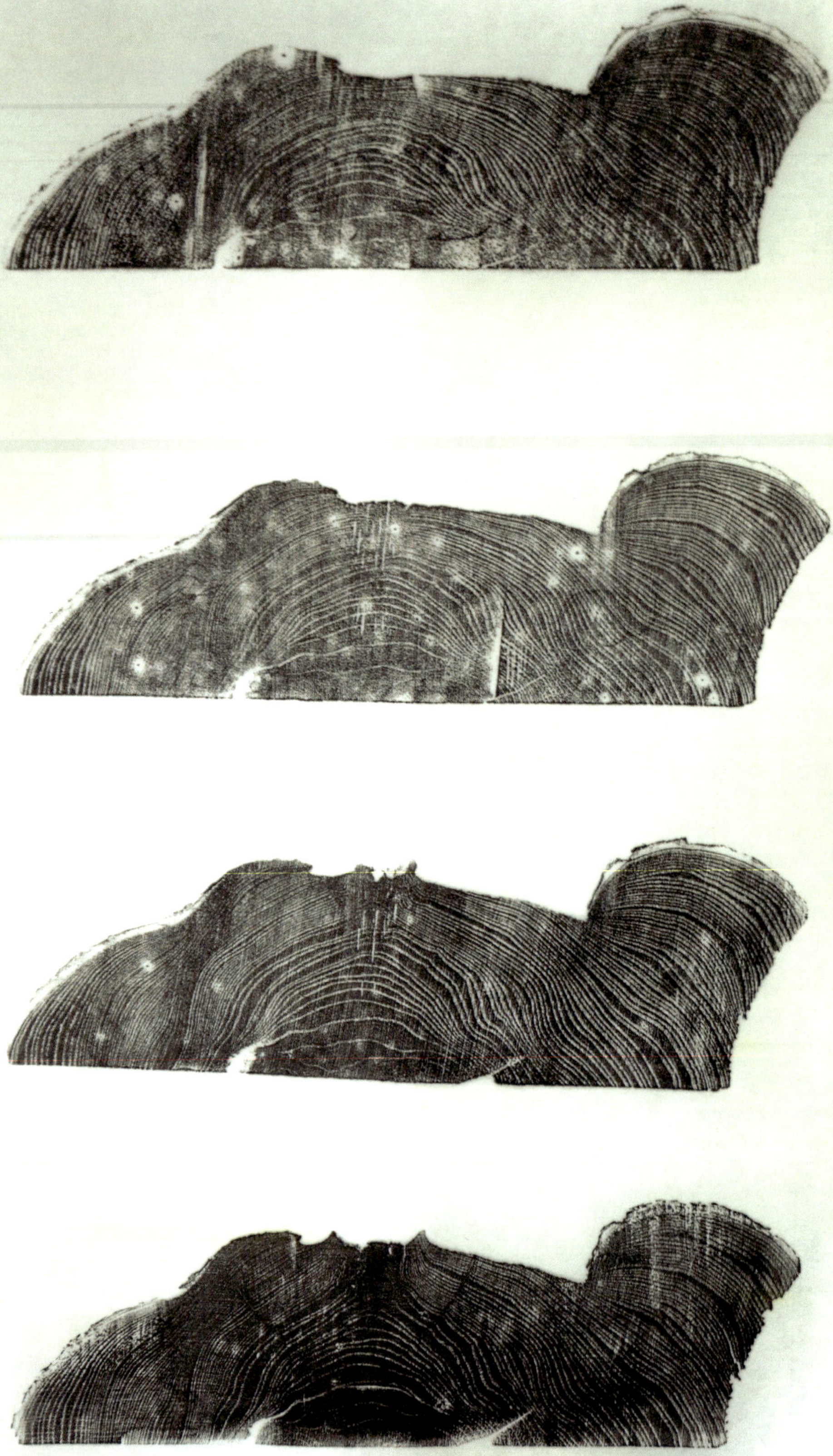

Tree Cookies

Eli Sobel

Fig. A
Catalpa

The scenery of the everyday is populated by trees. In Charlottesville, red maples, chestnut oaks, loblolly pines and yellow poplars are some of the supporting characters that make up the background of the city. As stationary observers, trees can be used as climate proxy data since their cores can provide indirect evidence of past climates. To express this data and distinguish between tree species, vertical and horizontal sections of these species have been turned into wood block prints. This process of felling, cutting, refining, planing and then printing from these samples makes their patterning legible. By making prints, the invisible is made visible.

Fig. B
Chestnut Oak

Fig. C
White Oak

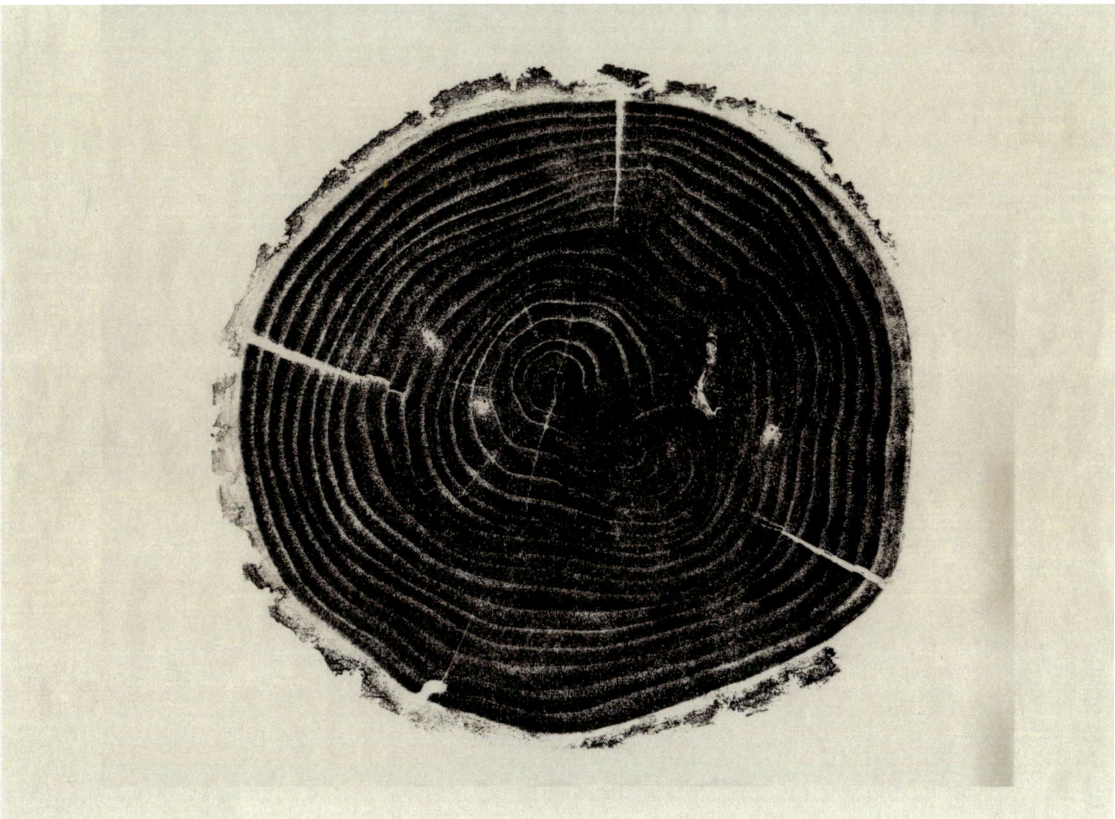

Fig. D
Siberian Elm

Fig. E
Loblolly Pine

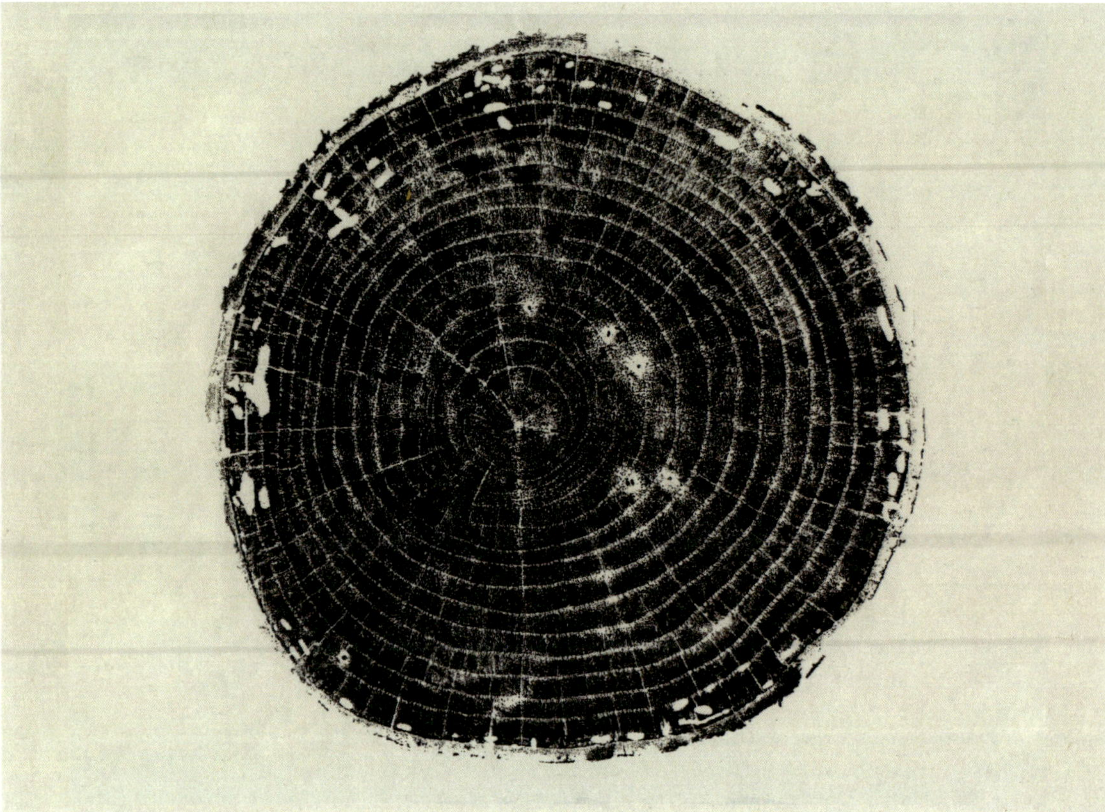

Fig. F
Black Locust

Fig. G
Ash

Fig. H
Printing tests of the tree species, Oak (left) and Loblolly Pine (right).

About the Author

Eli Sobel is a third year student in the UVA Master of Architecture program. Before attending UVA, Sobel worked as a letterpress printmaker, mold maker and visual artist. He has exhibited at Space Gallery in Portland, Maine and has been an artist-in-residence at MASS MoCA and Popps Packing. Sobel holds degrees in Fine Art from the Maryland Institute College of Art in Baltimore, Maryland and the Gerrit Rietveld Academy in Amsterdam, NL.

Ritual

Making [the] Everyday

Ariana Arenius

I remember asking my 엄 마 (umma / mother in Korean) why she continues to do the work that she does: "because I love seeing the joy it brings to people when they see something they love fixed and made new again."

My 엄 마 is a seamstress from South Korea who came to the United States over 30 years ago. Each day, she has and continues to be surrounded by a variety of clothes that need repair. I think of the times I would see her rethreading her sewing machine. The loud, ground shaking noises of the machine as she worked on repairing a well-loved shirt. The collection of every color of thread imaginable, assorted on the wall behind her as if it were a mural.

The following selected pieces offer a glimpse into the ways her everyday intersected with mine at a special moment in time. They were made in Professor Sanda Iliesu's course titled "100 Days of Making," a space where she invites students to pursue a craft of making every day for 100 days. For me, making went beyond the mindset of "I need to produce something" and became a process of exploring the deeper pockets of my identity and my connection to my mother.

Each day, I collected my materials — a needle, wool, and rice paper — and spent 30 minutes to several hours working. Early on, I expected a revelation or drive that would direct me towards exactly what to do and what to make. The reality was that I often felt lost at

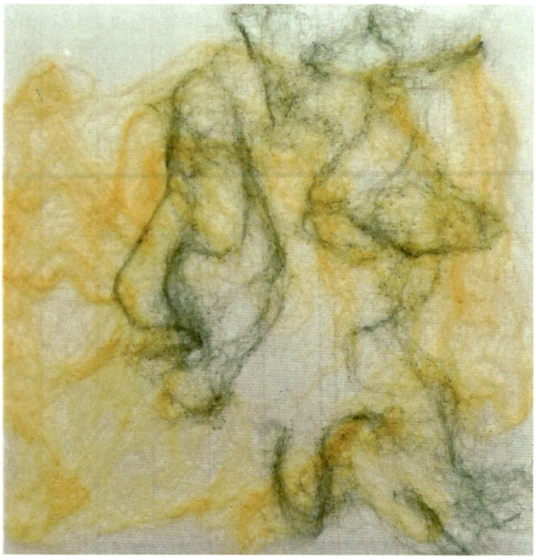

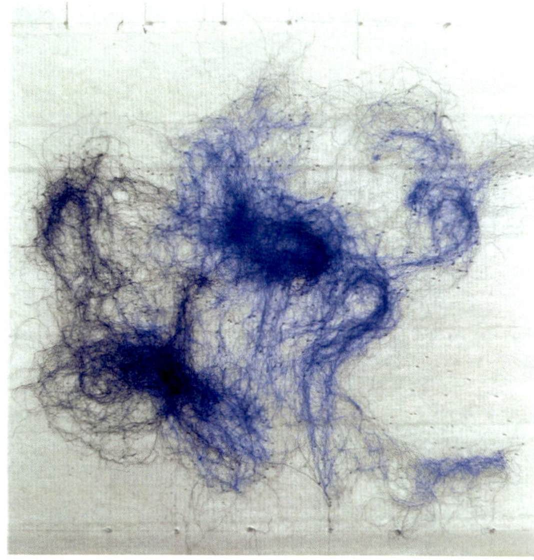

where to start and where to go – a feeling of isolation that I am sure many creative hearts unknowingly share.

Perhaps the looming pressures of wanting to make something exciting, new, or innovative were interrupting the creative energy that this project was asking for. As I reflect back, this was the first lesson that allowed me to let go of these unspoken expectations: making for the sake of making and nothing more.

To make also asks for a level of dedication — not only for a commitment to the process, but also a promise to yourself to be present in the moment and wherever it may take you. And in my case, an endurance to keep going for 100 days.

Making allows us to dream in a space that only exists within this process. We might feel compelled to wander in our thoughts, yet what continues to ground us in reality is the making itself.

I imagine the moments of both solitude and nostalgia my 엄마 experiences in her own process moving between dreams and reality.

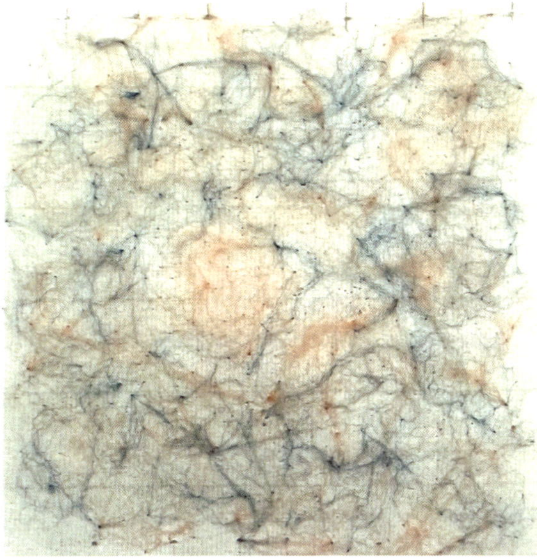

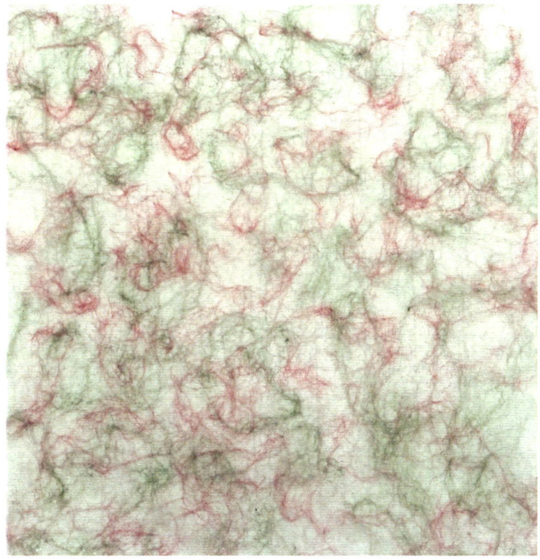

Making occurs not only in the present, but also in the past and in the future. Each time I picked up my needle, I was reminded of the times my 엄 마 did the same. There were moments when I would accidentally poke my finger and startle myself. I would look at my hands and think of my 엄 마's, remembering the times I would watch in awe seeing her hands move swiftly and elegantly. I thought about how they've changed since I was a kid — seeing a bandaid on one or multiple fingers, a pain-relief patch on her wrists, and now more often a wristband to help with arthritis.

The materials we use in making carry the ability to move us across time and space. Pulling apart the wool, it was as if I opened the memories of my 엄 마 sewing and fixing my stuffed animals, adjusting the fluffy white stuffing in each one. Her craft became an act of love and care without words, an experience many first-generation Asian Americans share. Making is bringing love and care into our everyday lives, whether it be for ourselves or for those around us.

Making reminds us to not forget where we come from and who has been a part of our story. This process connects me to my 엄 마 through the same movements. It becomes a way of making our presence known and keeping our stories alive. Each thing we do builds on the next, and carries forth each and every day.

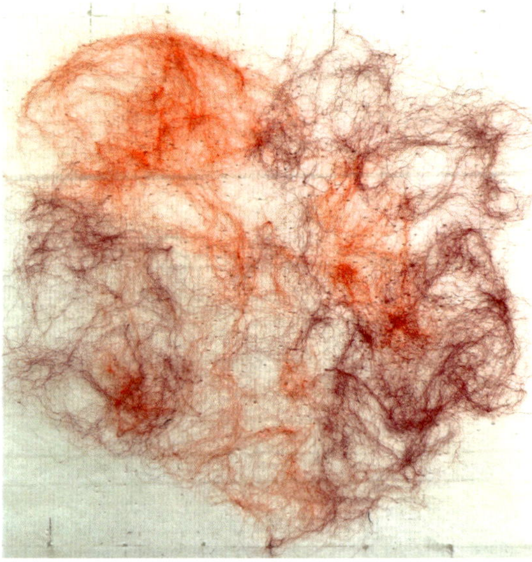

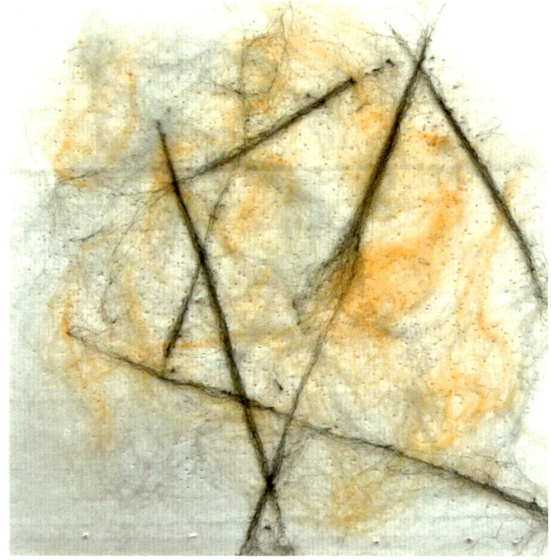

As I reflect about one process of making and the lessons that emerged, this visual essay, and love letter to my 엄마, also serves as a form of making. The words I use here and the stories I've curated are a part of my everyday life. They are deeply embedded not only in my identity, but how I interact with others in the world. To the patient reader: I hope that a strand of this story — a story of making and its musings — has found its way to your own.

About the Author

Ariana Arenius (she/her) is a landscape designer at Fall Line in Richmond, Virginia. She recently graduated from the landscape architecture program at the University of Virginia (2023). She collaborates on research projects in design pedagogy and pursues art through painting, drawing, and felting. She's drawn to the ways landscapes can be used as spaces of mediation, healing, and action, especially as a means of reclaiming power and crafting narratives. Arenius looks to the ways that her own cultural identity, as a first-generation Asian American woman, can serve as a lens for understanding complex intersections in landscapes that move beyond traditional binaries. Her studies have equipped her with strong sensibilities to speculate on the ways design can respond to our new and impending futures through collective action and care.

Contributor Biography

Sanda Iliescu (she/her) is a beloved professor of Architecture at the University of Virginia. Iliescu's practice spans the media of painting, drawing, and collage. Outside the studio, she makes murals and installations, some with students at UVA, where she is Associate Professor of Architecture. Molly Krom Gallery based in New York and Berlin, and Les Yeux du Monde Gallery in Charlottesville represent Iliescu's work.

Born in Romania, Iliescu received her BSE in Civil Engineering and M.Arch in Architecture, both from Princeton University. Her professional awards include The Rome Prize, a McDowell fellowship in painting and The Distinguished Artist Award of the New Jersey State Council of the Arts. Scholarly writing on Iliescu's artwork include essays by Carmen Bambach, Curator of Drawings and Prints at the Metropolitan Museum of Art in New York, and Paul Barolsky, Commonwealth Professor of Art History at the University of Virginia.

Photos by: Ariana Arenius

MENTATION
9
EPICERIE
VIANDE
DEPOT de PAIN
GAZ
JOURNAL
RETRAIT
BANCAIRE

Journal d'épicerie (2014)
on the merits of slowing down.

François Penz

The notes you are about to read – a sample from my *Journal d'épicerie* — can be construed as a museum of everyday lives, comprised of dialogues, people, objects, gestures, attitudes, and social behavior. These were collected over the course of six months in 2014, in a single location: a grocery store - *une épicerie* in French - situated in the small village of Fournès, 20 km West of Avignon in France. I gleaned everything that crossed my path, much like Godard who once said, 'in a film [...] I want to include everything, sport, politics, even groceries [...]' (Godard 1972).

The *Journal d'épicerie* consists of 104 entries, spanning eight months, written between April and October 2014. Together with my wife Fabia, we settled down in Fournès early February of that year; we were both on sabbatical, with high hopes of achieving a great deal of work, as one does. I had embarked on writing a monograph, along the line of a cinematic approach to everyday life in architecture (Penz 2018). I didn't have a detailed plan for the book as I favoured — and still do — a form of research that arises from within the very flow of writing, a process by which I gradually learn what I'm looking for...risky, but after all I had eight months.

However, just before leaving Cambridge, through a chance encounter (Penz 2018, pg. 1), I realised that Georges Perec's writing could become *le fil rouge* of my research. Perec had not only written a great deal in relation to the everyday — but he was also a filmmaker and had developed an original form of *écriture-cinéma* (Peytard 1997). While some of his work was already familiar to me, I plunged into his oeuvre with renewed interest, reading and collecting everything I could lay my hands on, while also watching all of his films. It is at the end of this process, which occupied the first two months of my sabbatical, that I formed the idea of the *Journal d'épicerie*. Fully under Perec's influence, I embarked in observing the world around me — reporting on my daily trips to the local grocery. This simple exercise, usually performed first thing in the morning, was instrumental in flexing my rather rusty writing muscles. Crucially, it heightened my fascination with everyday life, leading to a timely synergy between form (the act of writing), and content (the study of the everyday).

In the process of writing the *Journal d'épicerie*, I have invented nothing; I have simply been the secretary of my own observations. Yet I cannot claim it to be an objective document as I unavoidably reported only a fraction of what I saw and heard. And while I tried to be as factual as possible, it is an edited version of a self-ethnography, whereby I am also one of the 'actors'. My intention was to preserve a fragment of this unique period in my life, gleaning glimpses of people's lives whose paths I knew I would never cross again. Yet I was also aware that this diary was also part of my own history, a chunk of my own everyday life.

The *Journal d'épicerie* has laid dormant for nearly ten years. I recently reread it with pleasure, and in doing so I realised that I had forgotten many scenes and events. It brought back memories of my personal life as well as events that took place at the time, locally but also nationally and internationally. It is of its time in all its fastidious details. I was fully aware of Perec's advice to 'Note down what you can see. Anything worthy of note going on. Do you know how to see what's worthy of note? Is there anything that strikes you? Nothing strikes you. You don't know how to see. You must set about it more slowly, almost stupidly. Force yourself to write down what is of no interest, what is most obvious, most common, most colourless' (Perec 2008). This was partly an exercise in learning to observe – not a natural gift for most of us – but an essential one as emphasized by Eluard *'voir, c'est comprendre'* (Eluard 1939) [to see is to understand] — a crucial skill for architects and urbanists as 'In order to transform the city we must first observe it' (Abbott 1997). In my case, it was a limited form of spatial observation from the point of view of the people around me, mainly within the perimeter in and around l'épicerie.

L'épicerie was the setting for a diverse cast of regulars (actors), at times the same individuals and at times different ones, with Alain, the store owner, in the leading role, a constant presence, orchestrating everybody's comings and goings, day in, day out. I reported the actions and dialogues as faithfully as I could, often rushing home before it all evaporated from my memory. As well as the weather, I also recorded the journeys between my house and l'épicerie — a short two-minute walk — paying attention to changes if any.

A sample of the Journal d'épicerie is presented below. It is organised chronologically, and I have chosen five entries representative of a range of topics. It has to be noted that in the original diary I freely mixed French and English languages, but for the purpose of this article I have translated it in English.

THURSDAY 3 APRIL [FIRST ENTRY]

18.26 off to l'épicerie. Weather: overcast, drops of rains but mild around 20 degC.

A man and child walk are walking on the other side of our street... never seen them, I think...the parking by the church is full, four cars. There are twigs on the ground, Place de l'Église already noticed yesterday...odd as there are no trees around. Noise of a car behind me while walking down la Rue du General Gilly — but I didn't see the car.

Monsieur Charles is coming out of Alain's - he has a cucumber in his hand — I said 'hello' he said 'bonsoir'...I wondered why I said 'hello'. A woman is in the shop – I've never seen her before - wearing a grey raincoat, looking amiable...we say 'hello' — I ask Alain about the 'merchandise'... the radishes are here! But the lady helps herself first... 'there's competition' she says... Alain asks me if I'm going to bring some back to England... to plant them! Laughter ensues...I grab some organic radishes, two non-organic carrots, and a clementine... all for 3.86 euros... there are flowers, for the first time... 'but they're not edible because they're not organic,' says the lady... more laughter... but no croissants... 'a judoka came to get some fifteen minutes ago,' says Alain while yawning... he adds that the evening will be long. The lady comes back, she forgot her bread... a young man with a small beard enters, never seen before... he asks for locally grown asparagus... they're not available... 'there are organic ones'... no thank you he says... and on that I leave... Alain wishes me a good evening.

I check the notices in the shop window and on the side of the store… the poster for the Cirque Rasposo is displayed… we're going there on Sunday at the Pont du Gard. On the way back, I saw a young child and her older sister walking up Rue Haute… car noise in the background.

A cat is on a windowsill by the church.

18.38 back home.

FRIDAY 18 APRIL

Off to the shop – 9.30am – the weather is gloomy but mild.

I come across a cat…is it my 'cat'?

Alain is alone, fiddling behind his counter…I get some organic oranges, a croissant, a 'pain au chocolat', a salad…6 or 7 euros…I can't remember…we discuss the dorade [sea bream]…I confess that we overcooked it…Alain, a former chef, gives me a lecture on how to cook it, 'this poor creature died for nothing' is his conclusion… mine too. I ask about the Cyrano de Begerac play he saw last night… 'great, but too late…I was sleepy…we came back at 1am and I wake up at 4.30am…'. I meekly express some sympathy and then proceed to ask about his upcoming trip to Paris… 'this time we'll go to le Musée du Quai Branly…I am fed up with the Eiffel Tower'… in the meantime the blonde with the black car stops to buy 3 baguettes… 'do you want me to book you some bread on Monday… or are you out and about?' quips Alain with a smirk…'you know me well, on Monday I'm at the Feria [bull fight] in Arles!' [it's Easter Monday]…I leave.

Back home, Fabia asks about the strawberries [I forgot] and the zucchinis [I also forgot…too distracted by my conversation with Alain…and not on the list].

…I return to the shop, this time taking the stairs to the right of the church…for a change…in the distance, I see the woman who failed to get elected in the March municipal elections heading towards the shop, smoking…she greets me as I enter…Monsieur Kadder also enters, he had forgotten a can of lentils…I grab what's necessary plus a fougasse, following Anne-Marie's example…Fabia will be pleased, she loves fougasses!

9.50am I come back the 'normal way' and settle back home.

WEDNESDAY 4TH JUNE

11.20 am. off to the shop with my couffin [wicker basket] – grey weather.

I notice that there is a spare parking place... the cat strolls around the church square. I also cross paths with a young boy on a scooter, wearing a yellow T-shirt and a green helmet; he greets me. There's some activity on Rue de l'Endronne and Place Gilly – workers are pulling cables from the ground – fibre optics coming to Fournès?

Alain is in conversation with the man from the bar. Alain, to whoever will listen, advises against attending the Feria [bull fight] in Nîmes this weekend – too many people – and he doesn't like seeing animals killed but doesn't mind eating bull meat, if need be. The man from the bar mentions "...a good 'gardanne' nonetheless..." [a dish made with bull's meat] – on this note, the kiné [short for kinésithérapeute] arrives — "I hate the ferias...when I was young, I wanted to do ballet, but my very traditional father enrolled me in a folkloric group...we wore these big Provençal skirts...we were sweltering...I can no longer stand the sight of the Provençal fabric...and as for animals, I like to see them free." The conversation shifts to politics – the kiné despairs about the National Front's score [right wing political party] –"Half of Fournès voted for the National Front!" — sighs all around – a man arrives, I've never seen him before, asking for bread, "...no more bread...I had too many losses last week, so I reduced my orders..." explains Alain. In the meantime, I pick up a nice marmande tomato, two black krim tomatoes, some dish soap, and two organic zucchinis...I pay, 10.06 euros...two men arrive, one of them with a splendid white moustache, they seem to be delivering what looks like dry cleaning — I leave...Alain and the kiné continue to chat...

...the cable workers are having a conversation nearby...11.40 am, back home...still one spare parking spot.

FRIDAY, JULY 18TH

off to the shop at 9am — the morning fog has cleared, now warm and sunny.

...the car park is still full...in Place de l'Église, there's a house for sale sign, opposite the church...the bin lorry has come by, the street is full of debris.

In the shop, a woman I don't recall seeing before is there with her grandson, busy choosing some sweets...an old man with a white moustache also enters...I've seen him a few times before, usually in a dirty shirt, shorts, and slippers...quite friendly, he's grinning all around...the lady greets him, "Bonjour Marcel...hot, isn't it? You need to use the air conditioning." Marcel shrugs, "Yes, a bit. It only lasts a month..."...a young man enters, in a hurry, he goes ahead... then I encourage Marcel to get served while I am looking for fly catcher strips at the back of the shop...he engages Alain in an animated conversation about the type of lamb Alain could get him for next week, "I can't promise anything, but if I can, I'll get you a cassette...12 euros per kilo, there's a bit of everything...navarrin, chops...and soon it'll be the end of Ramadan...there will be tons of lamb"...he grabs a loaf of bread, pays by card, and withdraws some cash...he leaves, and in comes the man with the goatee...then a burly, tattooed guy who parks in front...never seen him before...we let him go ahead...he withdraws some cash and Alain hands him a 10 euros note, and leaves... goatee man proceed to ask if we could also been given 10 euros...we all laugh...I grab some chocolate, fly catcher strips, a paillasse [bread], two croissants, and a cucumber...8 euros...my fly catcher strips intrigue the man with the small beard, "...I don't have any flies..."...that in turn leads to an animated conversation about pollution, the man exclaims excitedly, "Pollution is terrible". Last night on TV, they showed glaciers all black, I'm telling you, all black." I let them continue, I pay, and I leave...

...in Place de l'Église, the woman with the black car closes the garage doors, we greet each other.

FRIDAY 3 OCTOBER [LAST ENTRY]

11.45 I step into our street in glorious sunshine.

On the way down to the shop, I come across Véronique Boudineau chatting with a girlfriend.

Alain is on his own...since it's my last visit I ask if I could take a picture of him in front of the shop...he graciously agrees and I take a few snapshots...he gestures towards the other side of the façade...if I come back next summer, it would all be changed... 'the entrance will be the other side'...we go back inside and I grab some organic apples, organic fennel, and organic muscat grapes... Thierry Boudineau arrives...we shake hands...he picks up a pack of beers and as he is about to leave, he asks if I would stop by to get some wine, but I reply that our car is now fully packed...he leaves...I shake hands with Alain and we wish each other good luck...a moustached man arrives...I leave and walk back up, for the last time, to Place Gilly, Rue de l'Endronne, and then Place de l'Église, finally reaching the house on Rue du Jeu de Mail.

Looking back on the diary, I realise that it is made of moments of almost unmitigated reality, inevitably edited and partial, but with very little of myself, in terms of my own emotions or judgements. As an observation of the everyday, it is essentially Perecquian, typical of the infra-ordinary (Perec 1989) approach. By contrast, Annie Ernaux's own approach in her *Journal du dehors* – not that I would want to compare myself to her — contains a myriad of insightful and personal touches, that elevates it to a literary oeuvre 'I sought to practice a sort of photographic writing of reality, in which the encountered existences would retain their opacity and their enigma [...] But in the end, I put much more of myself into these texts than I had intended: obsessions, memories, unconsciously determining the choice of words, of the scene to record' (Ernaux 1997).

I have long used a scene in *Smoke* (Wang 1995) as a paradigm for the idea of urban observation. In turn, I felt that for a short while, I had become Auggie, the character played by Harvey Keitel, whose hobby is making photographic recordings of his Brooklyn Street corner every morning at eight o'clock. In one of the scenes, Auggie advises his friend Paul (William Hurt), who quickly flips through his photographic records 'You'll never get it if you don't slow down, my friend [...] They're all the same, but each one is different from every other one. You've got your bright mornings and your dark mornings. You've got your summer light and your autumn light. You've got your weekdays and your weekends. You've got your people in overcoats and galoshes, and you've got your people in T-shirts and shorts. Sometimes the same people, sometimes different ones. And sometimes the different ones become the same, and the same ones disappear'.

Slowing down to take the time to note and observe the world around me, was good advice. It allowed me to move forward with my project. By the time I was back in Cambridge, I had completed the first draft of my book. As for the grocery store, Alain retired in 2016. It changed ownership but unfortunately it is now permanently closed, likely a victim of the pandemic. In a sense, my diary serves as a tribute to it, an immaterial *lieu de mémoire* (Nora 1989).

References:

Abbott, Andrew. "Of Time and Space: The Contemporary Relevance of the Chicago School." *Social Forces* 75, no. 4 (1997): 1149–82. https://doi.org/10.1093/sf/75.4.1149.

Eluard, Paul. *Donner à Voir.* Paris: Gallimard, 1939.

Ernaux, Annie. *Journal du dehors, Collection Folio Texte intégral 2693* (Paris: Gallimard, 1997), 9 – 10.

Godard, Jean-Luc. *Godard on Godard: Critical Writings.* Edited by Jean Narboni and Tom Milne, Cinema Two Series (London: Secker and Warburg, 1972), 239.

Nora, Pierre. "Between Memory and History: Les Lieux de Mémoire," *Representations*, no. 26 (April 1989): 7–24. https://doi.org/10.2307/2928520.

Penz, François. *Cinematic Aided Design: An Everyday Life Approach to Architecture.* First edition. New York: Routledge, 2018.

Perec, Georges. *L'infra-Ordinaire, La Librairie Du XXe Siècle.* Paris: Seuil, 1989.

Perec, Georges. *Species of Spaces and Other Pieces.* (London: Penguin Classics, 2008), 50.

Peytard, Jean. "De l'écriture-Calligramme à l'écriture-Cinéma: Le Cas Perec." In *Le Cabinet d'amateurs - Revue d'études Perecquiennes*, no. 6. Presses universitaires du Mirail-Toulouse, 1997.

About the Author

François Penz is an Emeritus Professor of the Department of Architecture and a Fellow of Darwin College, University of Cambridge. His AHRC project 'A Cinematic Musée Imaginaire of Spatial Cultural Differences' (2017-2020) expanded to China and Japan in particular many of the ideas developed in his monograph '*Cinematic Aided Design: An Everyday Life Approach to Architecture*' (Routledge 2018). He recently co-edited '*The Everyday in Visual Culture: Slices of Lives*' (Routledge 2022). As part of his practice based research, he runs film & architecture workshops in Venice, at the Architecture Biennale (2021) and the European Cultural Academy (2022), as well as at the British School at Rome (2023).

HONEYCRISP
TOTAL

Seeding Pedagogies
Mutualist Futures x Design

Emily Wettstein, Emma Potter, and Alex Daley

Setting the Table

Fig. A
Each element within the elaborately set table served a unique pedagogical function.

On a crisp and sunny spring evening, one hundred students, faculty, staff, and friends of the UVA School of Architecture gathered at a long and elaborately laid outdoor dinner table for the 2023 Benjamin C. Howland event. The dinner table became the site of a pedagogical experiment, reimagining the traditional lecture format to critically engage with the future of the discipline of landscape architecture, as projected through its pedagogies.

Pedagogy became a subject of design, as radical landscape educators, Nocturnal Medicine, MK Smaby, and Maria A. Villalobos H., guided guests through three "courses" — in the sense of successive dishes in a meal, a series of learning exercises, and alternate routes of action. Centered around the apple as botanical muse, each course was cooked and prepared by organizers and speakers, in collaboration with student organizations, modeling mutualism and interconnectivity in both content and method.

Course I
Deconstructed Apple Pie

Fig. B
The every day space of the North Terrace was temporarily transformed.

Nocturnal Medicine
"Dessert Play: A Pedagogical Reverie"

The first course was dessert, led by Larissa Belcic and Michelle Farang Shofet of Nocturnal Medicine. Guided by their "Pedagogical Principles" focused on sensual awakening, play, and experimentation, guests slowly immersed themselves in the smells, sounds, textures, and tastes of a deconstructed apple pie. Each guest then employed their "sensory research" to design the perfect bite for their neighbor. Upon receiving this carefully crafted "gift," participants were asked to consider what their collaborator was teaching them about flavor and pleasure. Starting the meal with an emphasis on embodied knowledge and an atypically vulnerable act of intimacy began to dissolve the traditional hierarchies of design education.

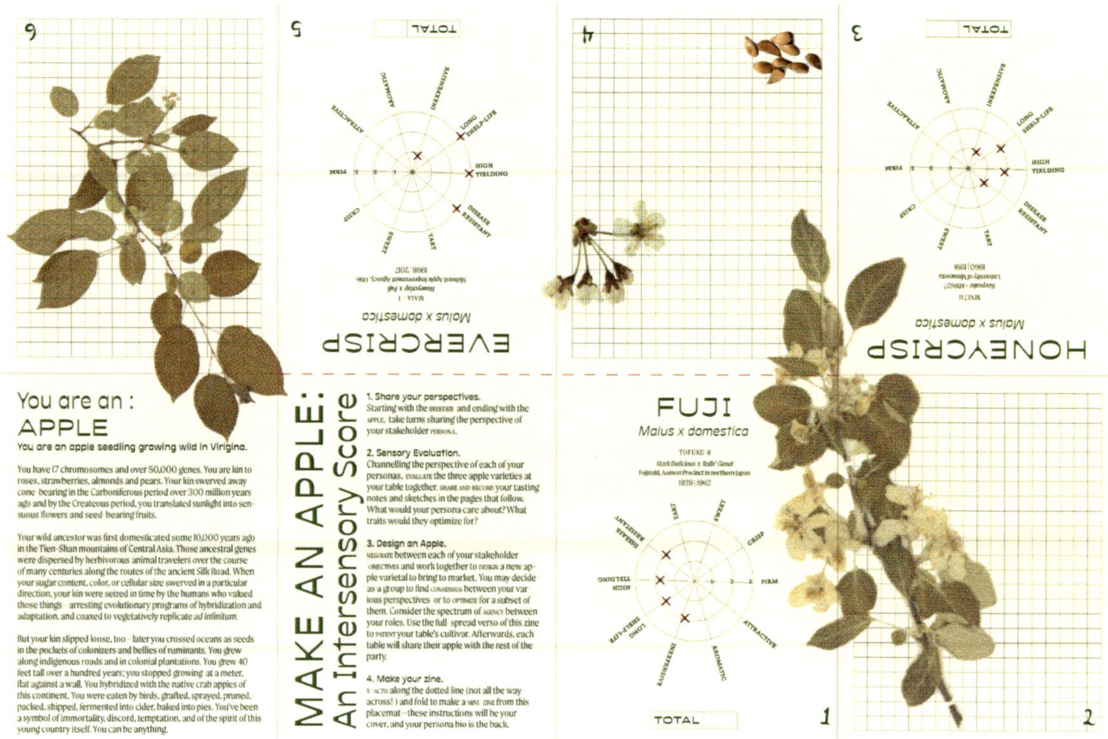

Course II
Beet, Apple, and Pea Shoot Salad

Figs C+D
Make an Apple: An Intersensory Score placemat and worksheet.

MK Smaby
"Make an Apple: An Intersensory Score"

In the main course, MK Smaby employed the "prepared environment" of the dinner party as the primary mode of instruction. Through the design of the sensory, social, material, and spatial environment, she invited guests to enter the lifeworld of the apple and to understand apples as thoroughly designed by committee. Then, each taking on a different persona with their own priorities and desires, guests negotiated the collaborative design of a new apple cultivar, helping foster an intimate understanding of the complex intermingling of values ever present in design.

COLOR	
S/P MATRIX	
MORPHOLOGY	
PROFILE	
ROOTSTOCK	
TOTAL	

NAME YOUR APPLE

NAME YOUR ORG

HOW TO MAKE AN APPLE

Tally up the average of your table's SENSORY— PERFORMANCE score from the EVERCRISP apple. Your table's cultivar design on this page may *meet* but *cannot exceed* that number. You can gain back or lose points from this total through your selection of COLOR, MORPHOLOGY, and ROOTSTOCK.

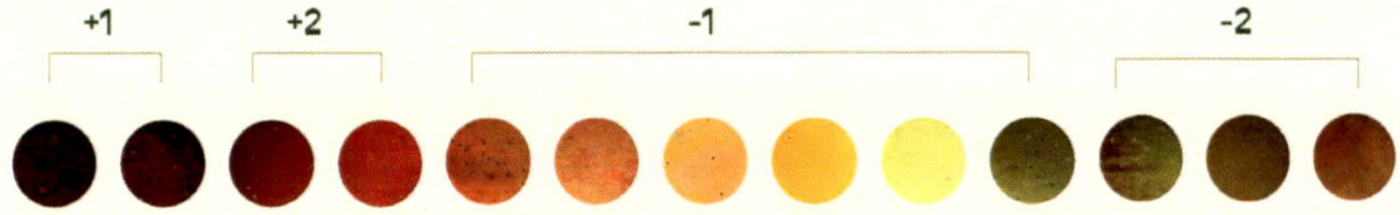

FRUIT COLOR

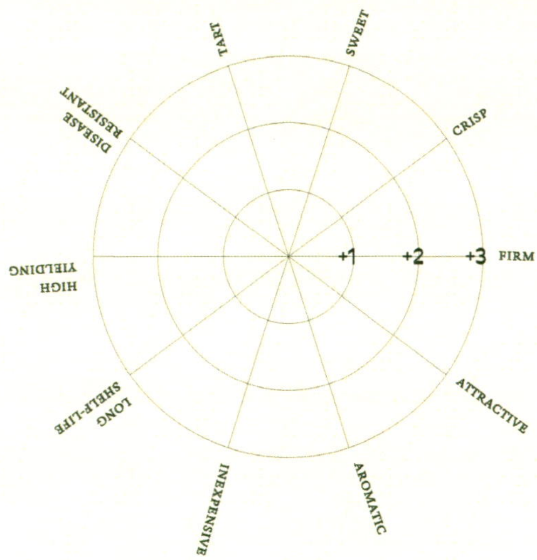

SENSORY PERFORMANCE MATRIX

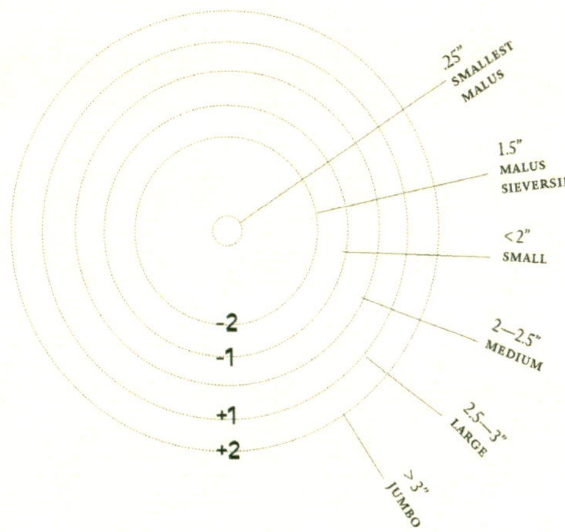

POME MORPHOLOGY

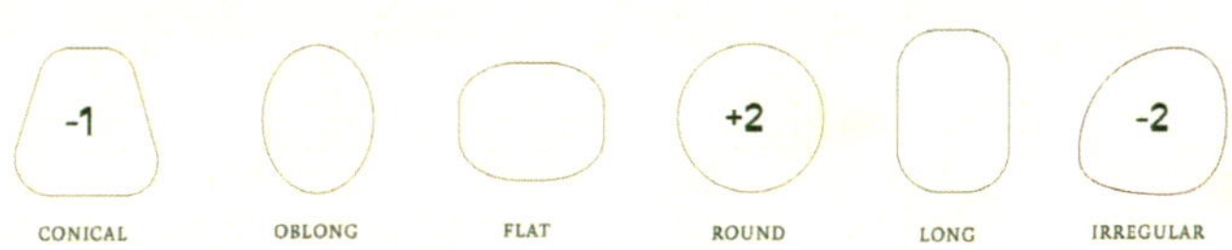

FRUIT PROFILE

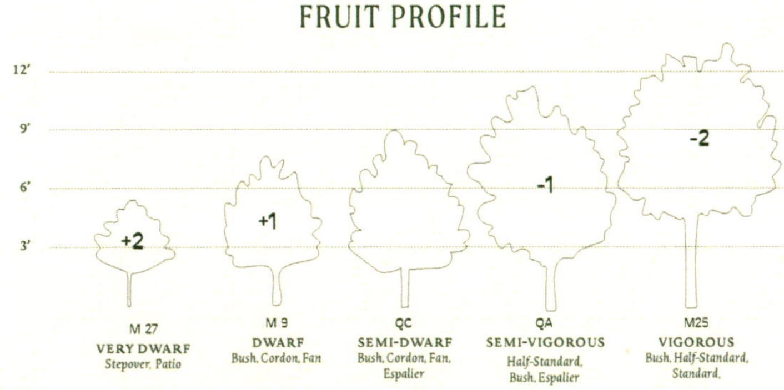

ROOTSTOCK

Fig. E
Participants test three apple varieties utilizing a Sensory Performance Matrix.

Course III
Chilled Green Apple and Cucumber Soup

Dr. Maria A. Villalobos H.
"Where Apples Grow"

The final course further expanded in scope and scale, as Maria A. Villalobos H. guided guests in collectively designing an anti-colonial botanical expedition in search of an apple. An outpouring of creativity immediately followed, as participants employed their prior sensory research and intersensory scoring to develop detailed stories and colorful expeditions. The tablecloth became an evolving atlas of speculative scenarios, spatializing the many ways in which our embodied sensory knowledge and experience manifest in our global networks.

Fig. F
The evening's sensory revelry resonated beyond the immediate event.

Clearing The Table

Fig. G
The evening's designed one hundred foot-long table on Campbell Hall's North Terrace.

As the night slowly came to a close, drawings, empty glasses, and apple cores remained as artifacts of the event. Flowers that decorated the tablescape were gently placed in student-made memorials, as gifts for Devin Chandler, Lavel Davis Jr., and D'Sean Perry. Finally, students and faculty worked together to clear the table leaving only the memories and co-constructed knowledge they embodied. The event was an exercise in collaboration, in which a broad cross-section of the department came together to reframe the most everyday act of making, sharing, and eating food into a radical pedagogical experience.

About the Authors

Emily Wettstein is an Assistant Professor in Landscape Architecture at the University of Virginia School of Architecture. Her current research projects share a foundational grounding in marginalized sites and subjects. In one, she seeks to co-construct inclusive design pedagogies from landscape architecture's core concepts and methods. The other, researches the potential of liminal sites to facilitate critical confrontation and dialogue.

Emma Potter is a third year Master of Landscape Architecture student at the University of Virginia. Prior to UVA, Emma attended Virginia Tech where she studied environmental policy and planning and became keen to community engagement and systems thinking approaches. Community engagement events, such as the Howland lecture series, drives her passion for curating genuine experiences for people and other species.

Alex Daley is in her second year of the Dual Masters of Landscape Architecture and Architecture at the University of Virginia. She is passionate about designs that center care for all involved. Before coming to UVA, Alex attended New York University's College of Arts and Science where she studied Environmental Studies and Italian. Over the past four semesters, she has explored environmental and human relationships in projects at multiple scales, from nature-based infrastructure to bus stops and student centers.

Photos:
Figs A, B, F: Emma Potter
Figs C, D: MK Smaby
Figs E, G: William Shivers

20-30 Minutes Everyday

Ryan Moody

In March 2020, our everyday changed. Although we did not know how long, devastating, or transformational the COVID-19 epidemic would be, we immediately knew that access to nature would provide an opportunity for stress reduction in the wake of disruption. We knew this because Moody Graham had spent the previous two years reviewing the foundational research and current studies supporting the understanding that time in nature reduces stress, restores attention, and promotes healing.

The mental and physical health of Americans has declined sharply over the past three years. Despite spending more money on healthcare per person than other nations, our collective health is failing — life expectancy in America is falling, suicide rates are rising, and teen mental health is in crisis. Landscape Architecture will not solve these problems. However, increased access to nature through carefully designed landscape architecture has the power to help. Our profession has a role and responsibility to help us heal.

Our research, evaluation of successful public and private spaces, and critical thinking about the role of landscape architecture, especially in relation to building architecture, led us to develop a series of design principles that we use to underpin our work. Many of these principles can help transform our everyday experiences of working, living, and being into more positive, peaceful, and healthy environments. Below are some strategies we have been thinking about, promoting through lectures, and employing in our work.

moody graham

Ryan Moody <ryan@moodyarchitecture.com>

MA WFH today - Friday 03/13

Ryan Moody <ryan@moodyarchitecture.com> Fri, Mar 13, 2020 at 9:23 AM
To: MLA design staff <pod@moodyarchitecture.com>

Pod,
Additional follow-up from our discussion yesterday.

1. DCPS closed schools starting Monday for two weeks. This is a good thing but I am not sure how it will affect Moody Graham yet (meetings may get cancelled, etc.)
2. Everyone is encouraged to tele-work. Use G-chat, telephone, email, free conference call, etc. to stay in touch. Please let me know if there are access issues with multiple people trying to connect. Meredith and Emily will likely continue to work from the office. Brittany, I see no reason for you to come in over the next two weeks. I will deposit checks as necessary and keep an eye on the mail. Please send out invoices if you haven't already.
3. Jay, please keep us posted on your trip and let us know when you need documents, prints, information, etc.
4. Next week looks like a good time to get any field work done- site visits, site documentation, etc.
5. **Please spend 1 hour each day over the next two weeks walking, jogging, sitting, etc. outside when feasible. Find a favorite park, trail, or arboretum, and use it as a respite. Put the time down as professional development.**
6. Let me know if there are any questions or concerns. I will setup a conference call for a Monday morning staff meeting at 9am and we can discuss further at that time.

Thanks,
Ryan

Ryan Moody | **Principal**

a: Moody Graham | 1318 H St. NE | Washington, DC
w: www.moodygraham.com
p: (202) 543-1286

Fig. A
Email sent to staff regarding COVID-19 and the importance of spending time outside.

WELCOME SUN AND AIR

Operable windows with shade controls can increase control and comfort, connect us to the exterior environment, and provide better air quality than mechanical cooling and heating. Sunlight affects melatonin production, sets circadian rhythms, and can influence serotonin levels. Reduced light exposure can result in circadian imbalance, which increases the risk for depression and disease (Kellert, Heerwagen, and Mador 2008).

BRING GARDENS INSIDE

Indoor plants reduce psychological stress, increase job satisfaction, lift mood, and improve cognitive performance. These effects can combat disease and chronic stress (Bringslimark, Hartig, and Patil 2007).

PLANT A TREE FOR EVERY WINDOW

Views of green landscapes improve cognitive performance, accelerate healing, and increase recovery from stress (Ulirch 1993; Li and Sullivan 2016). Properly sited buildings and carefully considered windows provide neurological nourishment.

ENRICH THE EDGES

Protected outdoor areas adjacent to buildings provide cover, transition, refuge, and environmental modulation.

OPEN VIEWS

Humans prefer prospect views that allow us to survey our surroundings for opportunities and hazards. We also have an innate desire to explore and appreciate mystery (Ulrich 1993).

SHAKE HANDS WITH PLANTS

When we know something, we are more likely to protect it. By making plants accessible and inviting, we provide opportunities to meet and appreciate them.

LAYER GARDENS

Vertically layered gardens create enclosure and immersion and attract the greatest number and diversity of wildlife. Tough and low-maintenance native plants capitalize on evolutionary symbioses with local fauna (Tallamy 2007).

EMBRACE SOFT FASCINATION

Non-rhythmic movement of light refracting off the water's surface provides soft fascination, resulting in mental regeneration. The presence of water has historically signaled the availability of drinking water, defensive advantages, and high food productivity, which may support the nearly universal positive response and a strong preference for visual access to water (Ulrich 1993).

PROVIDE PLACES TO SIT

A moment of refuge with a favorable prospect provides a moment of contemplation, rest, and recovery. Moveable furniture creates flexible use and gives users more control.

ENCOURAGE TWENTY MINUTES

Twenty to thirty minutes in nature provides maximum stress reduction in relation to time expended. Benefits extend to increased immune system resilience, reduced pain levels, increased serotonin levels, and improved cognitive performance.

REVEAL TIME

By highlighting the seasonal change of plants and materials' life cycles, we reconnect to our broader climate and context and expand our sensory experience.

Fig. B
Today, amid declining health, we know that time in nature makes us healthier and happier, but we spend less time outside — why?

MAKE IT BEAUTIFUL

Our efforts must be beautiful. They must attract our attention, promote wonder, weave the ground and sky, and change over time.

References:

Bringslimark, Tina, Terry Hartig, and Grete Grindal Patil. "Psychological Benefits of Indoor Plants in Workplaces: Putting Experimental Results into Context." *HortScience* 42, no. 3 (2007): 581-587.

Kellert, Stephen R., Judith Heerwagen and Martin Mador. *Biophilic Design: The Theory, Science and Practice of Bringing Buildings to Life.* Hoboken, NJ: John Wiley & Sons, 2008.

Li, Dongying, and William C. Sullivan. "Impact of Views to School Landscapes on Recovery from Stress and Mental Fatigue." *Landscape and Urban Planning* 148 (2016): 148-158.

Tallamy, Douglas W. *Bringing Nature Home: How Native Plants Sustain Wildlife in Our Gardens.* Portland, OR: Timber Press, 2007.

Ulrich, Roger S. "Biophilia, Biophobia, and Natural Landscapes." In *The Biophilia Hypothesis*, edited by Kellert, Stephen R., Edward O. Wilson, and Paul Shepard, 73-137. Washington DC: Island Press, 1993.

About the Author

Ryan Moody (MLA, MArch 2007) is a landscape architect and founding principal of Moody Graham in Washington, DC. Moody and classmates Matthew Ibarra (MArch 2006) and Kevin Bell (MArch 2006) started Lunch in 2006. Lunch was created to address a problem — the great work of other universities was on display through architectural journals at Prairie Avenue Bookshop in Chicago (closed 2009), but the University of Virginia School of Architecture was absent — why?

The Country of the Everyday

Amanda Coen

Fig. A
Snapshot from
Photo essay. Photo
© Amanda Coen

Tal como si el drama sísmico hubiera concluido al llegar a este extremo del mundo, solo ha quedado aquí, como recuerdo, un escenario de serenas proporciones, sin protagonistas y sin espectadores. En el continente de las locas geografías, la comarca uruguaya es como un remanso de las furias.

> *Just as if the seismic drama had concluded when reaching this end of the world, it only remains here, as a reminder, a scene of serene proportions, without protagonists and without spectators. In the continent of crazy geographies, the Uruguayan region is like a haven from the furies.*
>
> *Original quote in Spanish from "Anexo: De Las Cartas de Eduardo J. Couture a la Nación Uruguaya" that forms part of "Carta del Paisaje del Uruguay."*

A world apart defined by a very different passage of time, a haven amidst chaos. The geological history that defines the landscape could not be more adept to tell the story of much of what I have observed since the pandemic landed me in Uruguay. A landscape defined as "una penillanura suavemente ondulada" (a gently rolling peneplain) produced by fluvial erosion over a long period and undisturbed by tectonic shifts, Uruguay seems to have escaped the seismic disasters the pandemic brought upon a large portion of the world.

Fig. B
Uruguayan landscapes

A tiny, often overlooked country where "wows" are not offered on a silver tray. A place that requires patience to uncover the poetry beneath. The beautifully muted landscapes, the subtle hues, a lack of distinction between days, the casual cool that seems an innate part of the populace, so many things ever-so-slightly subdued. The beachgoers applauding at sunset (yes, I thought at first, the sun will go down again and they'll repeat tomorrow as if it's a surprise), the traffic-watching yerba mate-sippers, the gauchos on horseback monitoring the campo, the fishermen with their horse-drawn carts of fresh fish clapping in the driveway, the lazy dogs lounging in the road, the recycling of everyday goods to no end. A place where capitalism is kept at bay.

The time and space to evolve new processes and ways of working, to develop curiosities to immediate surroundings, to draw lessons from the landscapes that now define my everyday.

Author’s Note

I arrived in Uruguay in March 2020, a place where family histories seem to come full circle but under distinct historic circumstances. In the 1970s my mom made her way hitchhiking from Massachusetts to Uruguay only to find herself amidst a burgeoning dictatorship which would imprison several of her closest friends, forcing her eventual departure after two years. Friday the 13th marked my arrival, the day COVID made its first appearance in Uruguay and the rest of the world began to go into lockdown. I had spent the prior six weeks conducting research in Brazil with a grant from the Architecture League of New York, and was to stop in Uruguay and Argentina before returning to New York. However, all plans went on hold. What was to be a week in Uruguay, turned out to be the longest week of my life, having now extended into four years.

This piece is a reflection as I try to enunciate what draws me to this unique corner of the world. The scale of the country and its economic realities create limitations, forming an ethos that leans towards editing and revising that resonates strongly. Its strong social fabric emphasizes looking out for others over getting ahead. As a landscape architect operating from a place where the field is still in its nascent form, it is the subtleties that I aim to better understand and the lessons they speak to, especially in the face of climate change, and the need for a rapid shift in lifestyles and expectations.

About the Author

Amanda Coen is a landscape designer, photographer and writer who is driven by a desire to reconfigure human relationships to the surrounding landscape and resources and bring life to that which often remains hidden to the average eye. Whether in a remote setting or in the middle of a bustling city, consciously or unconsciously, she collects, captures and digests what she sees. Sometimes her reactions are expressed in writing. Sometimes in images and drawings. And other times, in built works.

Coen holds a Bachelor of Arts in International Studies with minors in Anthropology and Studio Art from Macalester College and a Master of Landscape Architecture from the University of Virginia. Her previous work experiences include Snøhetta, Agence Ter, and Aldayjover. She was the recipient of the 2019 Norden Fund from the Architectural League of New York for her project titled, "Contemporary Ruralities" which examined the local impact of Inhotim, a contemporary arts center in the rural mining town of Brumadinho, Brazil.

Coen is currently a consultant with WHY Architecture and is working on several independent projects including writing, research and drawings. Her research has led her to ongoing collaborations with Fibershed to reimagine the landscapes of agriculturally-based regenerative fiber systems in a regional context, using drawing as a tool for translation, communication and advocacy. She has taught landscape design studio at ORT University in Uruguay.

Photos by: Amanda Coen

saw claytonia leaves.
Has been a mix of 70+40 days! Skunk cabbage is out- what stunning colors!
PACKERA AUREA
2.26.20
Golden ragwort
3.27.23
Veronica persica
gnolia
5. 2018
wntown
parts of the flower
pink-white four petals
3.2.17
toothwort
Cardamine concatenata
ssilago farfara

The Perpetual Journal

Lara Call Gastinger

A perpetual journal is a drawing practice that helps you to slow down, connect with nature, tap into one's artistic potential, and develop wonder and curiosity. In this journal, each year's drawings comingle with those of previous years, creating a rich tapestry of observations through the changing seasons.

To create your own perpetual journal, find a blank sketchbook. Each spread represents one week in the calendar year, so you need at least 52 spreads. The first spread is usually labeled as January 1-7, then January 8-14, January 15-21 until every day of the year is included. Then, when the moment of inspiration comes, and something catches your eye on a walk, that word or drawing has a place to land in your journal. As simple as a twig, a berry, a petal or as complicated as a Joe Pye weed inflorescence, it is up to you what speaks to you.

If you miss a week, that is ok but continue turning your pages, adding as you begin to see new things. Before you know it, you will be back where you started, looking at the page that holds your first observation and you will be very excited to see your older drawing add something new to the same page but now a year later. As you continue in your perpetual journal, your skills of observation will become keener, you will become more curious, foster a deeper sense of wonder, and you will have an established practice of mindful nature connection.

Perpetual journal spread January 1 - 7, pen and watercolor on paper, 9 x 6 inches, 2022

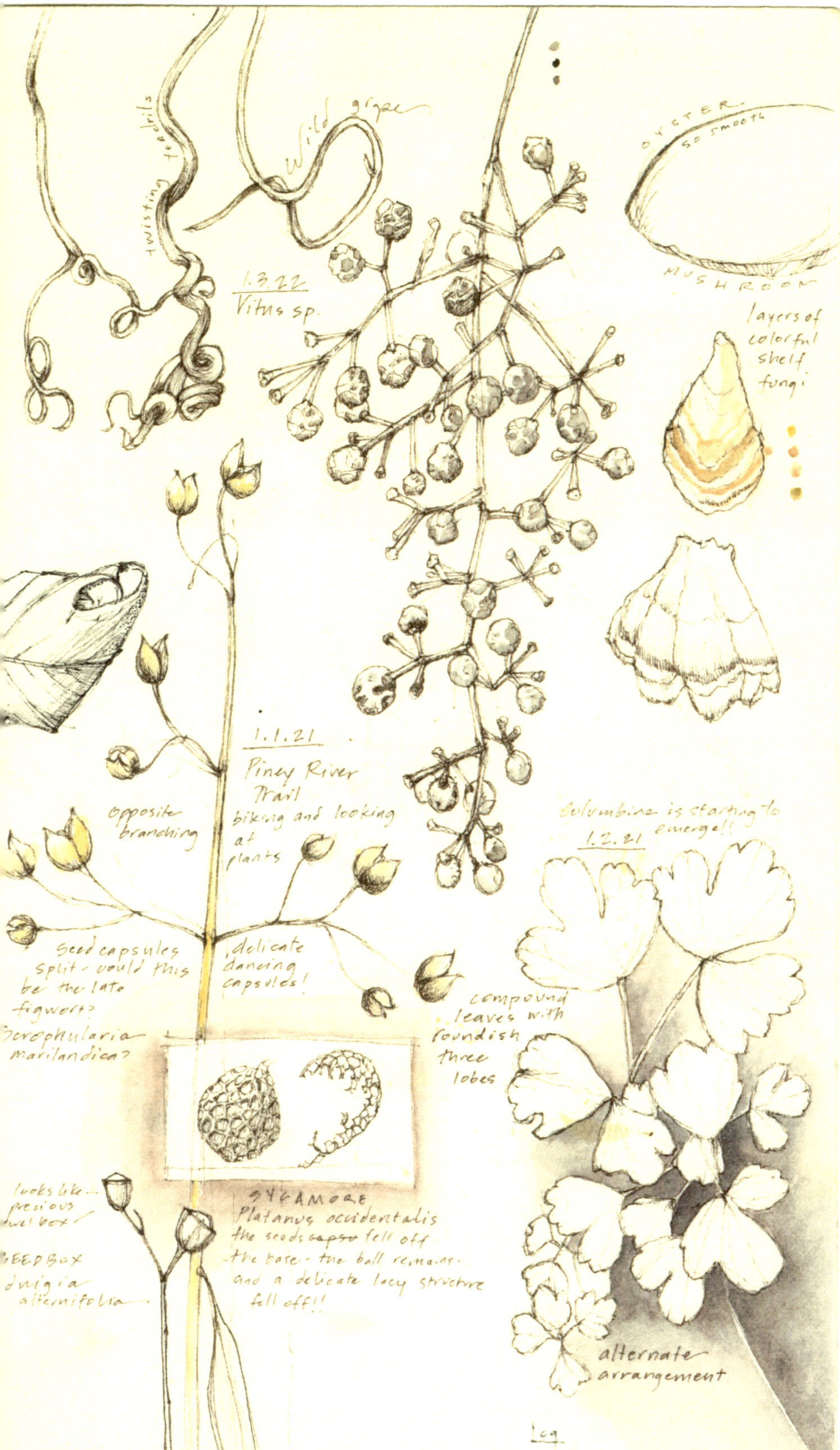

twisting tendrils
Wild grape
1.3.22
Vitus sp.
OYSTER
so smooth
MUSHROOM
layers of colorful shelf fungi
1.1.21
Piney River Trail
biking and looking at plants
opposite branching
seed capsules split - could this be the late figwort?
Scrophularia marilandica?
delicate dancing capsules!
Columbine is starting to emerge!!
1.2.21
compound leaves with roundish three lobes
SYCAMORE
Platanus occidentalis
the seeds fell off the base - the ball remains and a delicate lacy structure fell off!!
alternate arrangement

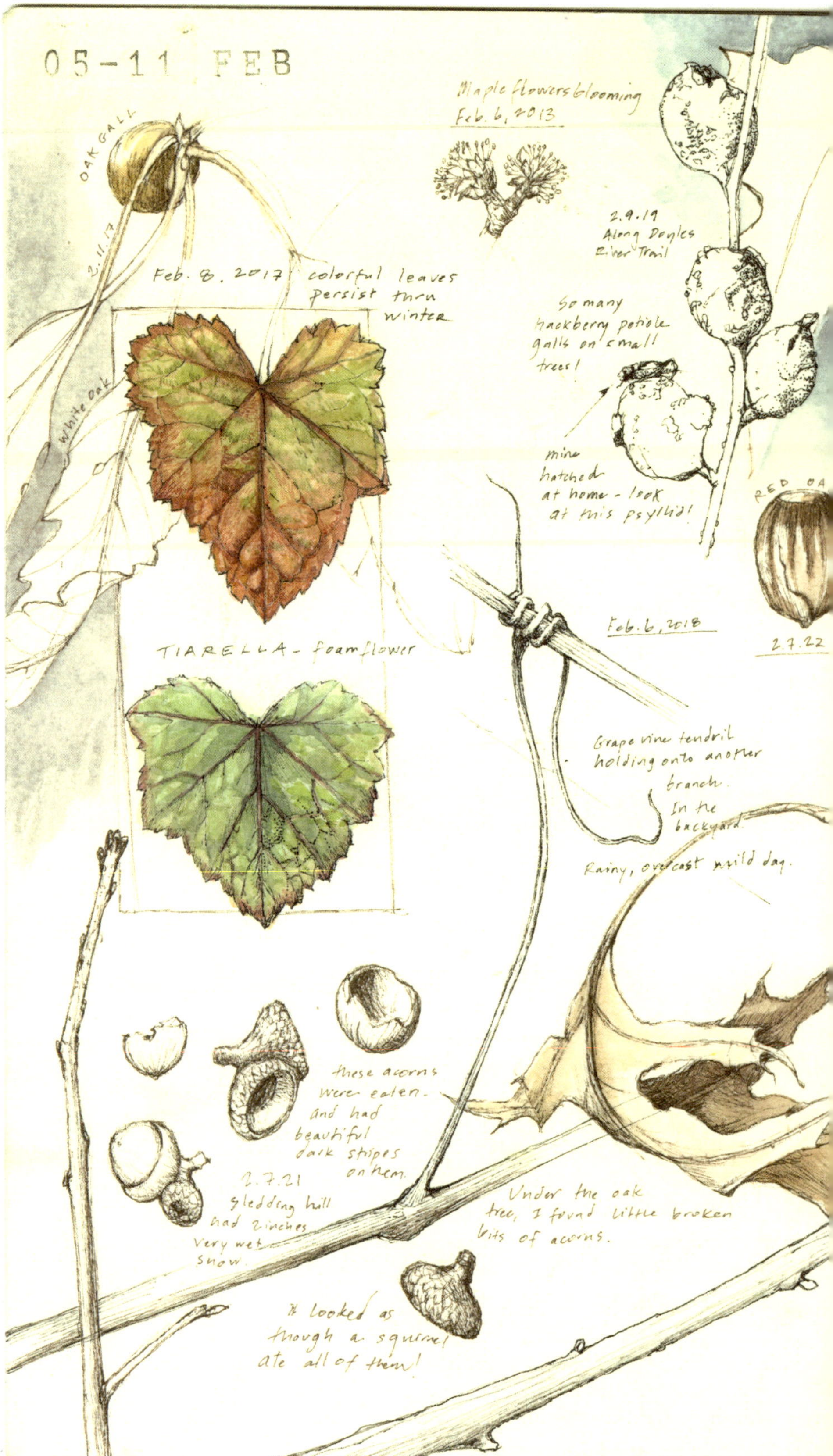

Perpetual journal spread February 5 - 11, pen and watercolor on paper, 9 x 6 inches, 2022

curled Sycamore leaves persist so long on ground!
2.5.19
Sycamore + grape vine along my run parkway.
petiole splits into multiple fibers and strands as it decomposes.
FUZZY!!
(SEEDS (ACHENES) HAVE ALL BEEN DISPERSED)
Feb. 5, 2017. Monticello, fallen branch
LIRIODENDRON TULIPIFERA
tulip poplar
2.6.16
rattlesnake plantain
2.6.22
numerous sycamore leaves fallen
2.9.20
bark with moss and lichen in beech forest
beautiful green clumps
striped wintergreen
CHIMAPHILA
Pawlonia tomentosa
Empress Tree
2.6.16

Perpetual journal spread February 26 - March 4, pen and watercolor on paper, 9 x 6 inches, 2022

3.2.2017
icebush buds enlarged.
Saw Claytonia leaves.
Has been a mix of 70+40
days! Skunk cabbage is
out - what stunning
colors!
2.26.20
PACKERA AUREA
Golden ragwort
3.1.21
Avens
basal rosette
backyard
glossy round
leaves
3.3.22 pubera
Stellaria media?
CHICKWEED
crawling along
the ground -
Riverview park.
3.2.17
toothwort
Cardamine concatenata
looks like
a strange
planet!
2.29.20
distinct buds
2.29.20
Patricia Byrom Forest
hike Zone 40
Grape fern
purple
colors
Sycamore
occidentalis
Platanus acerifolium

1.5.22 turkey tail
1.2.13
finding so many on decaying logs
1.2.19 McInnis Park
curling white oak
sunlight so brilliant.
grasses
Vaccinium sp.? blueberry
small holes in leaves
wild onion

About the Author

Lara Call Gastinger is an artist and botanical illustrator from Charlottesville, Virginia and was the chief illustrator of the *Flora of Virginia*, a botanical reference. She holds an undergraduate degree in Biology from the University of Virginia and a master's degree in plant ecology from Virginia Tech. She has been awarded two gold medals (2007, 2018) at the Royal Horticultural Society Botanical Art shows in London and her work is in the Hunt Institute for Botanical Documentation. Her artwork appears in the latest *Peterson's Field Guide to Mushrooms* and *American Society of Botanical Artists Botanical Art Techniques Handbook*. She has gained international recognition with the creation of her "perpetual journal" that she teaches to others.

The subjects of her art are artifacts of the natural world and reveal detailed evidence of the natural processes of growth, reproduction, and decay. She finds inspiration in a carrot that has gone to flower, a broken seedpod, twisted roots, or insect damage to a leaf. She strives to make a plant portrait in such a way that it reveals its character and uniqueness. Her focus on the small details and celebration of the everyday hopefully inspires others to look a bit deeper and linger a bit longer.

Photos by: Laura Gastinger

Overlooked

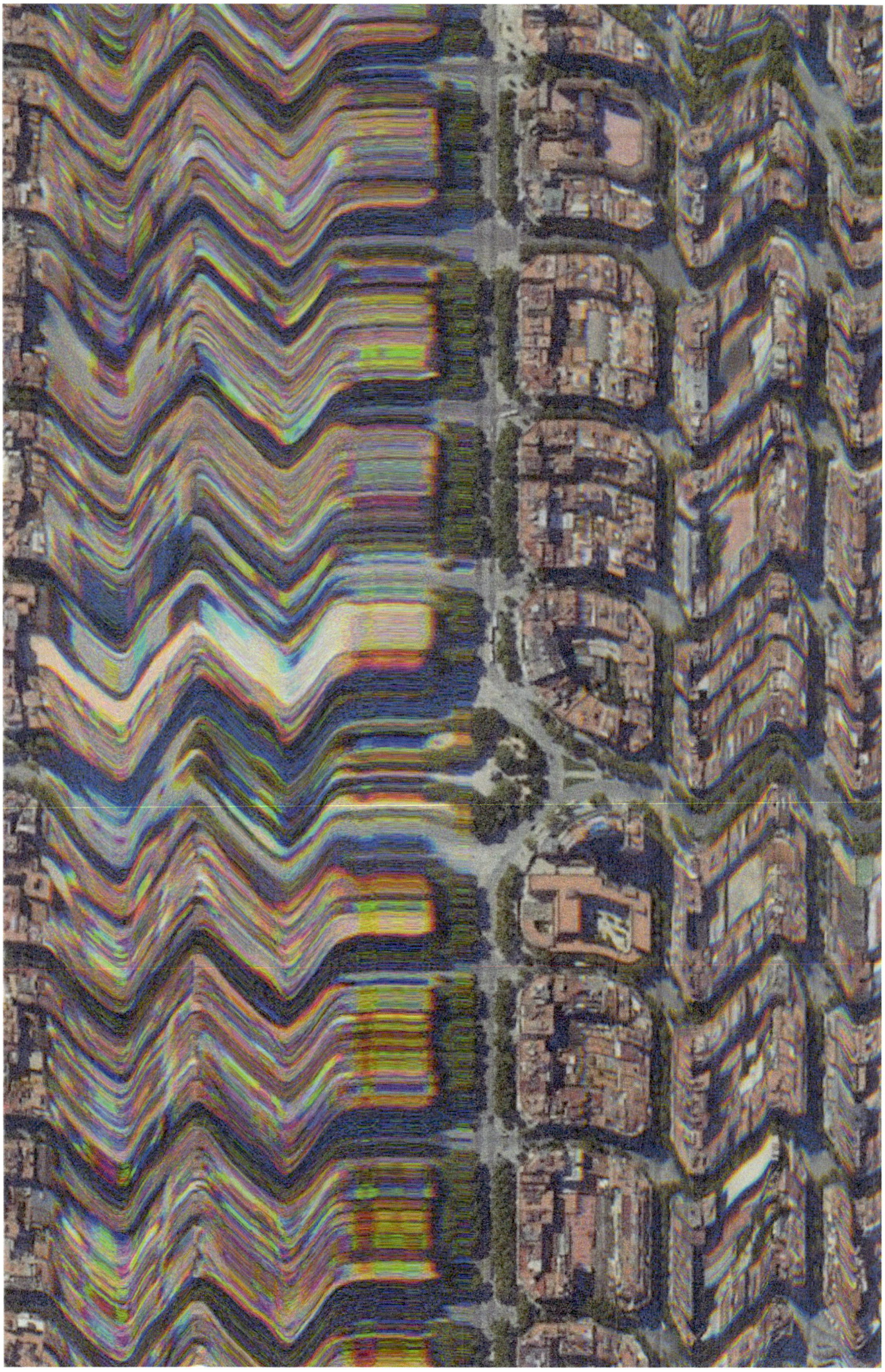

Everyday Dignity

Judy Shao-Yu Chen

The notion of everydayness is often associated with mundanity and triviality — chit-chat with neighbors, waiting for take-outs, getting groceries, walking the dog, picking up the kids, etc. As trivial as they may be deemed, the nothing-in-particularness is of great importance in fostering and solidifying the foundation of individuals' lives and the operation of larger society, and the spatial environment that accommodates these daily rituals deserves much more attention and thoughtfulness.

To accomplish everyday tasks requires our bodies to thread between public and private realms. And as a societal species that yearns a sense of belonging in both domains, weaving spatial designs in the urban fabric that bridges the two realms become essential in building a healthy public.

How can design extend that comfort and quality of life we build in private space into public space? How can the sequence of performing everyday activities be funneled and punctuated through design tactics? How can creating opportunities for lingering provide moments of respite and satisfy the need to observe and to be observed? How can design elicit dynamic varieties so that doing daily tasks is not simply going through the motions? What kind of design creates spontaneity in consistencies, activates diversions in repetitions, and establishes dignity through triviality?

Fig. A
Aerial photo of
Passeig de Sant Joan.

This essay examines Passeig de Sant Joan in Barcelona, Spain as a case study to probe how the design and deployment of a bench in a streetscape makes the quotidian act of sitting in public an act that bolsters the dignity of everyday life.

Passeig de Sant Joan is a street renovation project completed by the landscape architecture office Arquitectura Agronomia (led by Teresa Galí-Izard) with architect Lola Domènech. Extending more than 1km (0.62 miles) linearly on both sides of the avenue, the design enlivens the streets with ample lingering and walking space that interacts with other public programs and private restaurants' need for outdoor seating (Figs A+B). To explore further how the benches perform as a key catalyst of the space, this essay will approach an analysis of the bench design in three perspectives: 1) form and materiality, 2) marking/blurring boundaries, 3) deployments and space-making.

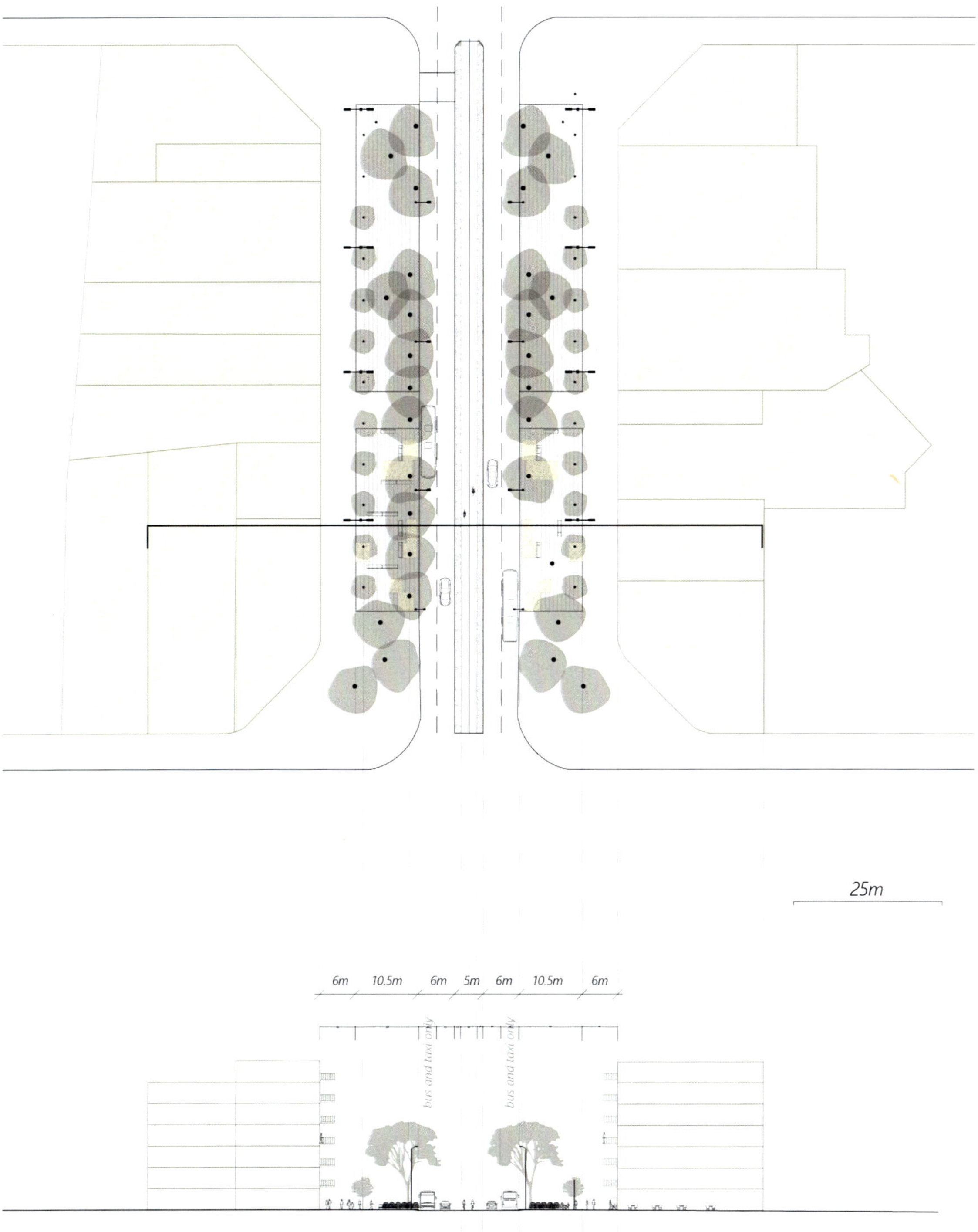

Fig. B
Streetscape section of Passeig de Sant Joan. In Barcelona, private vehicular traffic is spatially the least prioritized in Passeig de Sant Joans, yielding ample space for bikers and public transportation and granting dignity to the daily habit of walking, sitting, and lingering in public.

0.65m
2.13ft

3m
9.85ft

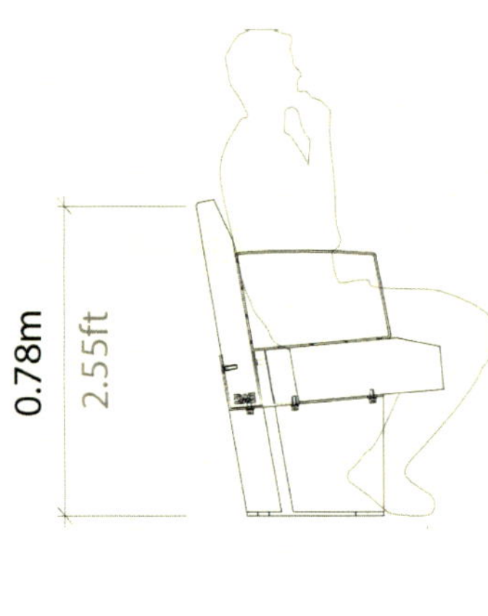
0.78m
2.55ft

Fig. C
The smoothness of the oiled pinewood allows all ages of users to engage with the bench safely and comfortably. And never underestimate how many ways a bench can be used.

Fig. D
Measured drawing of the Sumo bench. The ergonomic design and material choice allows human bodies to linger in comfort for longer periods of time, bringing in static activities among the bustling foot and vehicular traffic.

Form and Materiality

The bench "Sumo" used in the entire streetscape project is a design by DAE Escofet1. The first impression of the bench is the visual and physical weight it has: thick slabs of oiled finished pine wood and sleek steel handrails dividing the bench into uneven-spaced seats. The design allows joining multiple unit benches into one continuous long bench, allowing diverse variations in seating arrangements. The benches are placed at varying distances between 0-3.5m (0-11.5ft) from the pedestrian walkways, removing the bustling disturbance of foot traffic. The light brown color of the pinewood pops out in the street's green and gray backdrop, sending clear visual invitations to passers-by.

The durable quality of the bench elevates the seating experience compared to the flimsy and choppy park benches we usually see in public parks in the United States. The ergonomic angle of the benches alleviates the stiffness of the material and supports the body comfortably. (Figs C-E)

Whoever takes the seat will feel respected and valued. It's not a bench for desperation or lack of choice, it's a formal invitation to pause for a moment and enjoy.

ESCOLA
MOZ-ART

Fig. E
Larger groups such as teenagers, delivery services waiting for orders, and friend groups of all ages can easily find bench configurations that fit their group's needs. Individuals can also occupy a bench with a sense of belonging, being alone together.

Making/Blurring Boundary

Passeig de Sant Joan utilizes benches to mark edges, placing them against planting beds, restaurants' private seating, and playground fences (Fig. F). The benches' thickness becomes a barrier when demarcation of boundaries is needed, but at the same time it creates occupiable surfaces that transform a dividing boundary into a shareable space.

Placing public benches adjacent to restaurants' privatized seating space blurs the boundary between the private and public realms and catalyzes the integration of the two (Fig. G). The close vicinity of the bench to restaurants' seating allows public users to blend in with the diners who paid to be in the space. The durability and beauty of the public bench obscures the discrepancy that we often see in privatized public spaces — private seating using nicer furniture circled around by curated planters versus an unappealing and patchy public bench standing alone or shoved in as an afterthought among other public facilities on the street (Fig. H).

Fig. F
The bench is incorporated as part of the playground fence, creating appropriable boundaries.

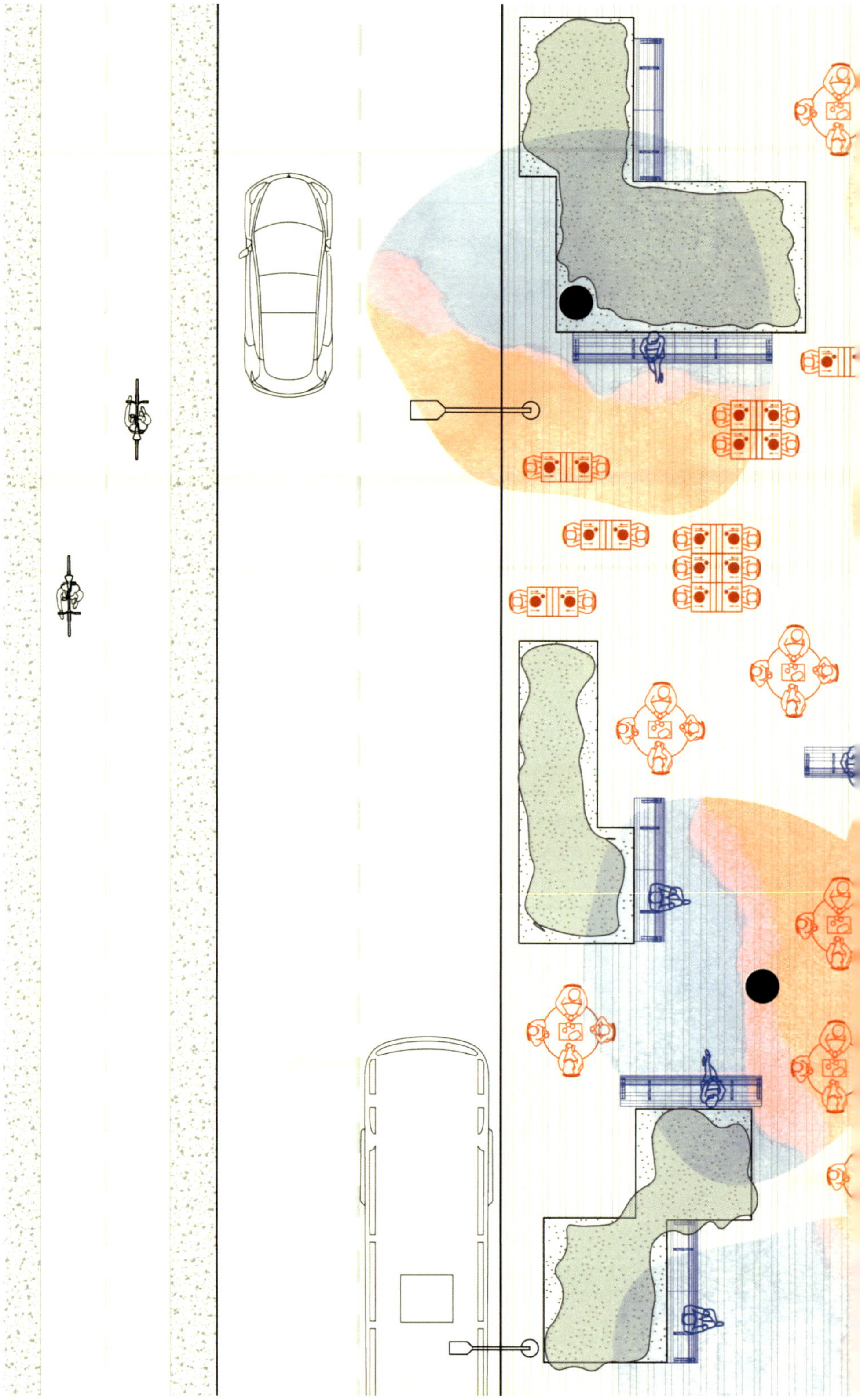

Fig. G
The proximity of public and private seating blurs the boundary between public and private realms.

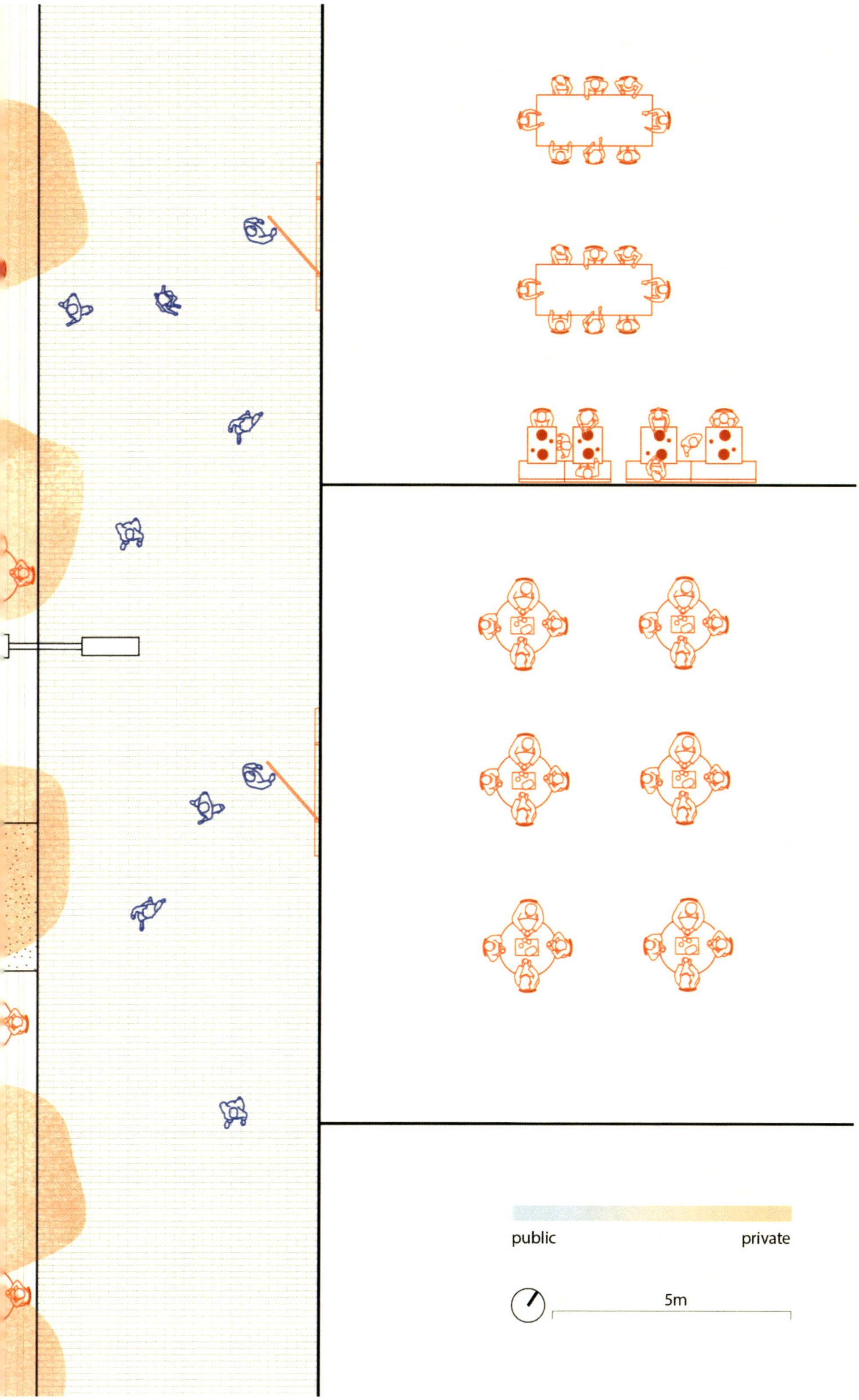
public
private
5m

Fig. H
The public bench users are as entitled, at ease, and comfortable as the restaurant diners.

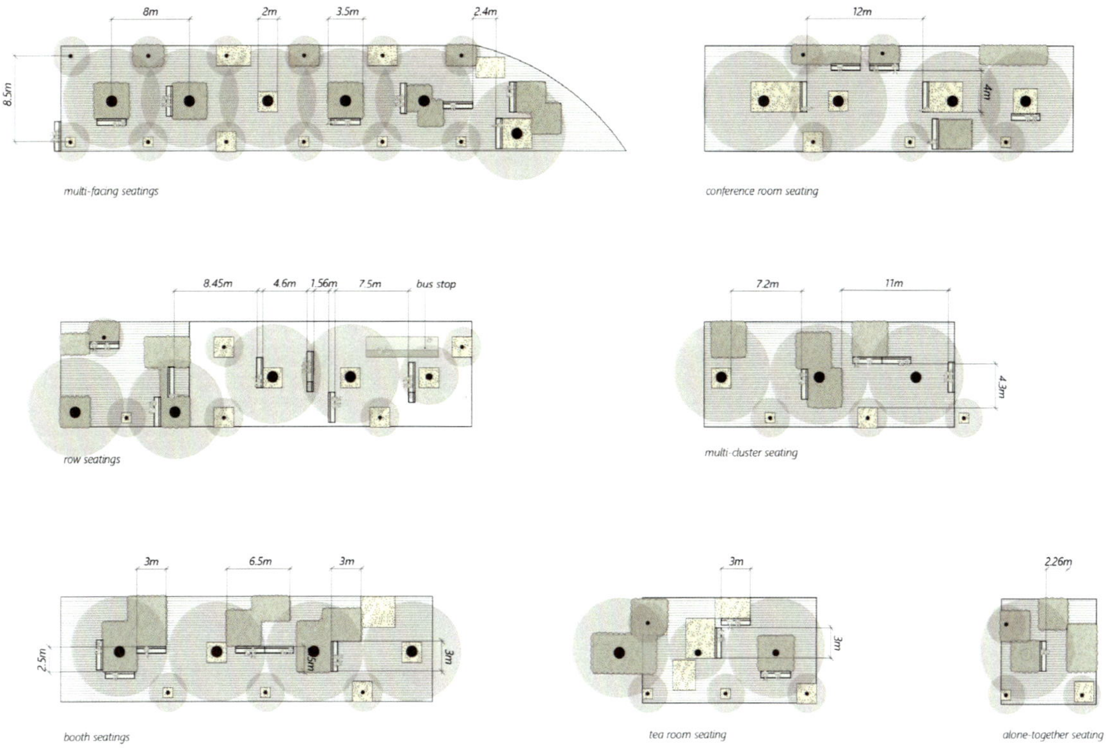

Fig. I
The configuration of vegetation with benches creates distinct room types, providing a spectrum of private — public experiences along the 1km long street.

Deployments and Space-Making

There are three main types of vegetation on Passeig de Sant Joan: 1) thick, waist-high shrubs that buffer the vehicular traffic from the pedestrian space 2) small understory trees dotting the edge between walking space and lingering space, and 3) large canopy trees staggered from the small understory trees providing shade and using tree trunks to structure the rhythm of the street. The benches are arranged in concert with how the vegetation is deployed and create rooms with different levels of openness and enclosure, allowing people looking for seats to pick an experience of their liking. (Figs I-J)

Inhabiting public space as the routine of everyday life is a celebration of humanity, interweaving and exposing ourselves to the larger collective to feel significant, connected, and seen.

Passeig de Sant Joan epitomizes the potency of multi-scalar design thinking in public space: a single bench displays individuality, and clusters of benches and plantings orchestrate collective motion; a single bench interweave the paths of individuals, and a systematic configuration of benches and vegetation harmonizes the flow of public and private realms and generates gradients of in-betweens.

Passeig de Sant Joan supports the desire for exposure and the yearn to blend in, reminding us that all activities are equally entitled to occupy public space, and everyday ventures are quintessential to enliven the landscape.

Fig. J
Contrasting experience of openness (see bottom left + right photographs) and enclosure (see top left + right photographs).

About the Author

Judy Shao-Yu Chen holds a bachelor's degree from the National Cheng Kung University in Taiwan where she studied Foreign Language and Literature with a minor in Urban Planning. She then moved on to University of Virginia for her Master in Landscape Architecture and was named UVA's 2023 Olmstead Scholar. Her research focused on projects that attended to climate resiliency, public space inclusivity, and urban design strategies that mend fragmented spatial fabrics.

延郡会馆
潘捷会馆

Revaluing Tea Shophouses

Zhouhan Li

Tea shophouses [Cha-Chan], mostly found in port cities like Fuzhou and other inland tea-production villages, refer to a spontaneous way of using a residential building to accommodate tea production and trade activities.

Some were originally residential buildings transformed into tea shophouses by adding mezzanines and ladders, while others were purpose-built tea shophouses that retained traditional timber frames and courtyard architectural forms.

The interweaving of production, trade, and domestic life puts forward unique spatial operational systems, often employing shared space usage at varying times of the day and vertical division of different functions. These spaces exemplify how traditional courtyard residences have been ingeniously repurposed to meet the evolving demands of trade.

The following pages explore two of these shophouses and examine their spatial arrangements that melds together domestic and commercial everyday life.

Shengshun Tea Shophouse

The well-preserved "Shengshun Tea Shophouse" located at No. 238-240 Xiahang Road, Fuzhou, stands as a testament to the illustrious history of Ou-Yang's Family in the tea trade. In its entirety, the residence was initially designed with the consideration of accommodating tea activities within the household, resulting in an organic interconnection between both production and daily living aspects.

As the era of robust commercial development emerged, there arose entrepreneurs fully dedicated to business and production, prompting the emergence of mixed-use dwellings like the "Shengshun Tea Shophouse." Within such abodes, the emphasis on residential functions gradually yielded to commercial pursuits. These functions were sometimes positioned in the last section of the building and, at times, extended to the second floor during a period marked by significant commercial growth.

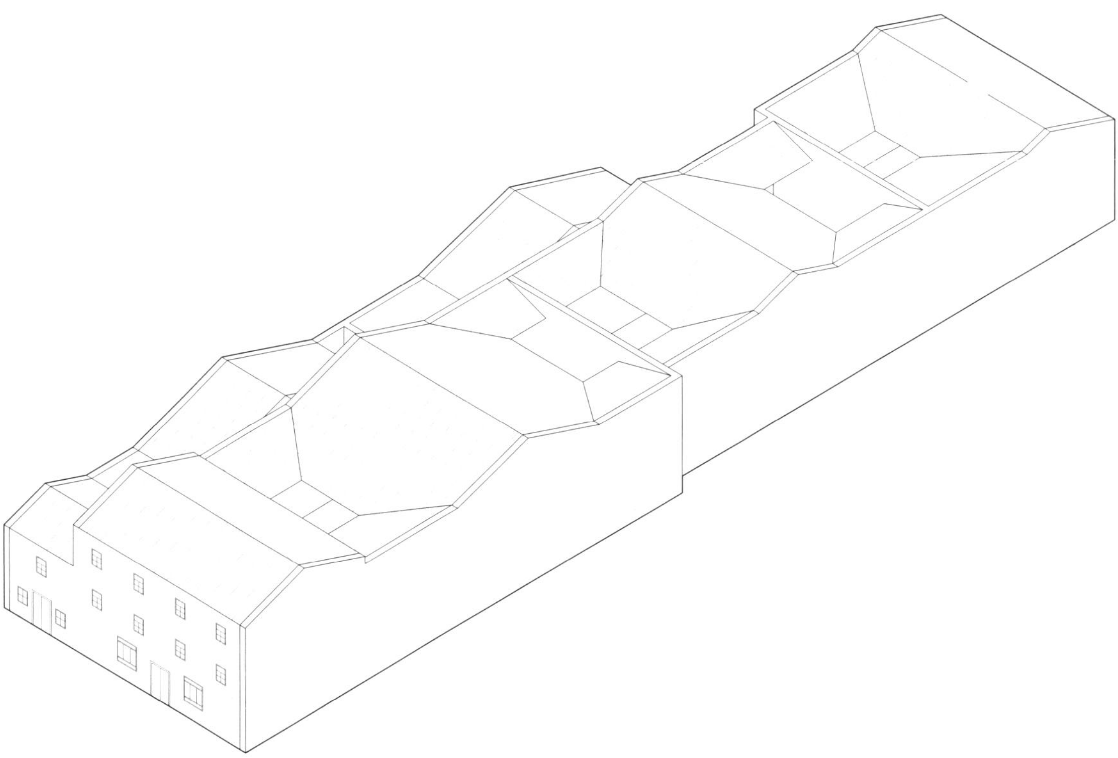

Tea Weighing and Collection

Due to the initial construction process accounting for larger-scale production needs, adjacent to the main tea shophouse, a two-story shed is specifically built for tea weighing, collection, and processing activities.

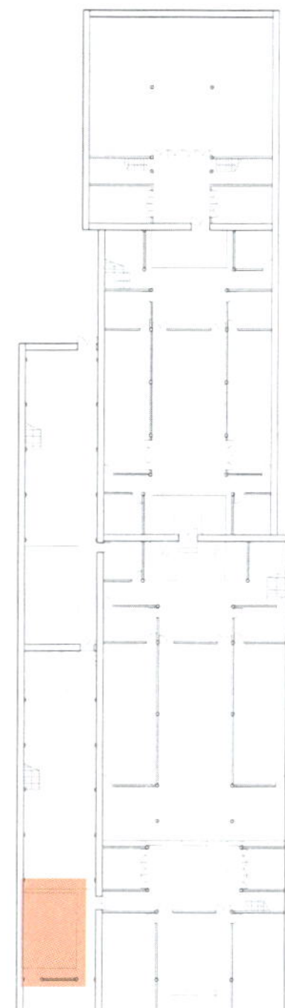

Tea Processing

Unlike early tea shophouses transformed from residences, which utilize the same space at different times or vertically separate different functions through the addition of floor plates, the functional division of the "Shengshun Tea Shophouse" is predominantly manifested in its plan layout.

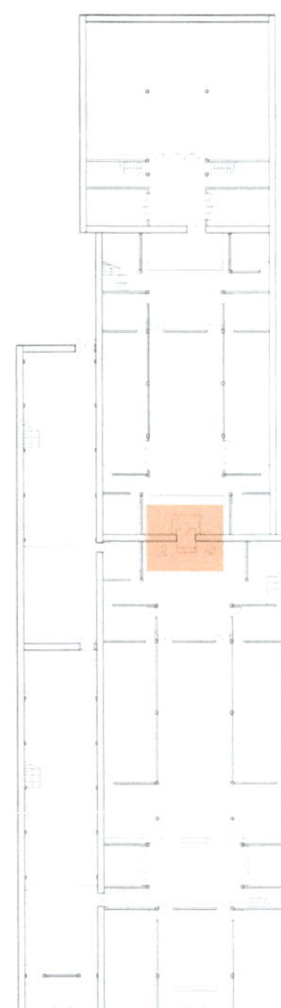

Main Trading and Living Hall

The main hall is a multi-functional space serving both tea trading and domestic ceremonies.

As a well-decorated double-height space, it highlights the significance of the tea trading process. Also, it serves as a hub for various activities reflecting daily life's essence, social interactions, and cultural practices. In this versatile area, families gather for meals, ceremonies, and celebrations.

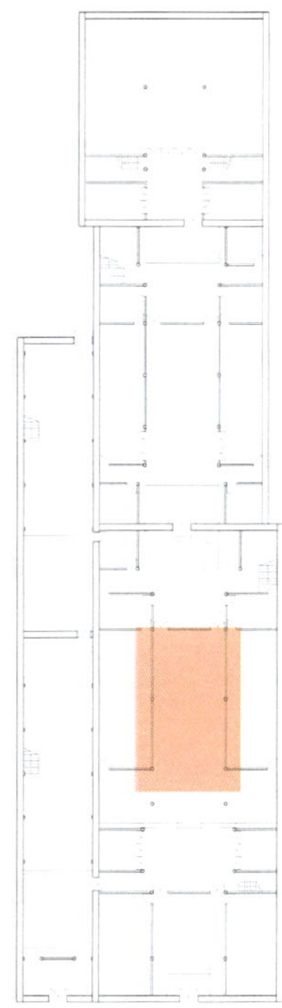

YuTongYong Tea Shophouse

YuTongYong Tea Shophouse is a representative example of handcrafted processing workshops for Anhua dark tea during the Ming and Qing dynasties, serving as a significant tangible embodiment of the enduring history of Anhua dark tea culture.

The existing main building comprises the main hall, east and west wings, main gate, warehouse, and courtyard, spanning approximately 43 meters in length and 35 meters in depth. The main hall houses the owner's office, accounting room, tasting room, and weighing room. The left and right wings, as well as the upper floor, serve as the production area. The courtyard measures 13.5 meters in length and 12.5 meters in width, paved with bluestone slabs.

Currently, it can still function as a workshop for the production of dark tea or a TikTok E-commerce Center. Apart from the front wall being replaced with red brick, the rest remains relatively intact.

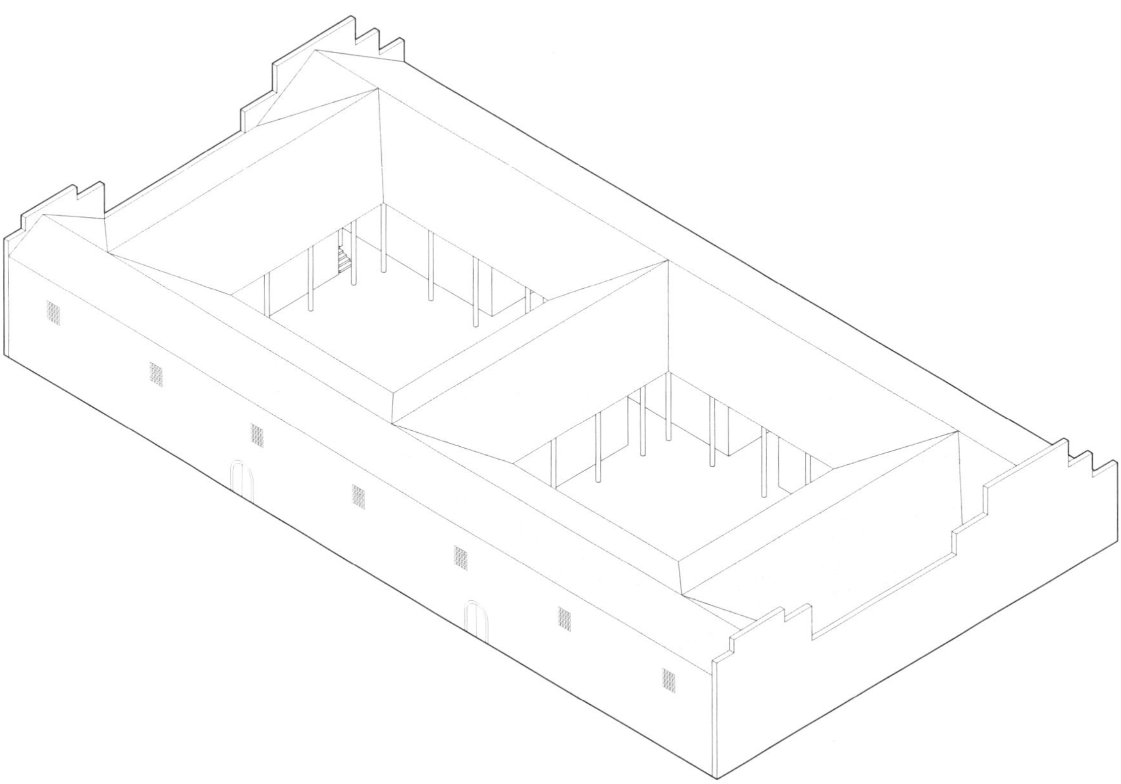

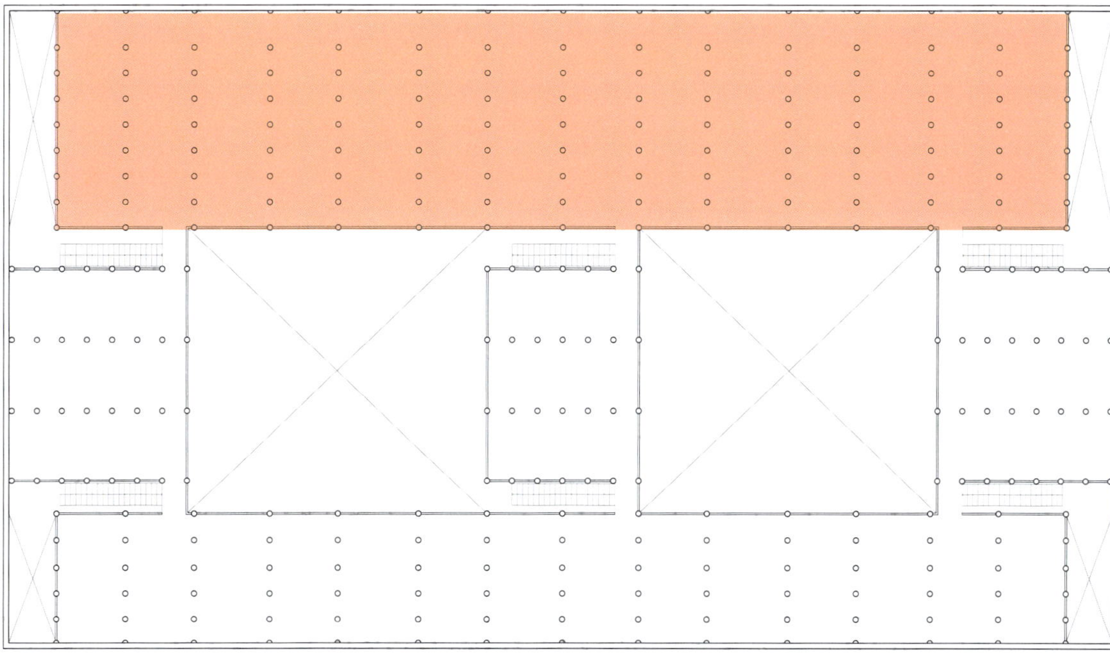

Large Space for Tea Processing

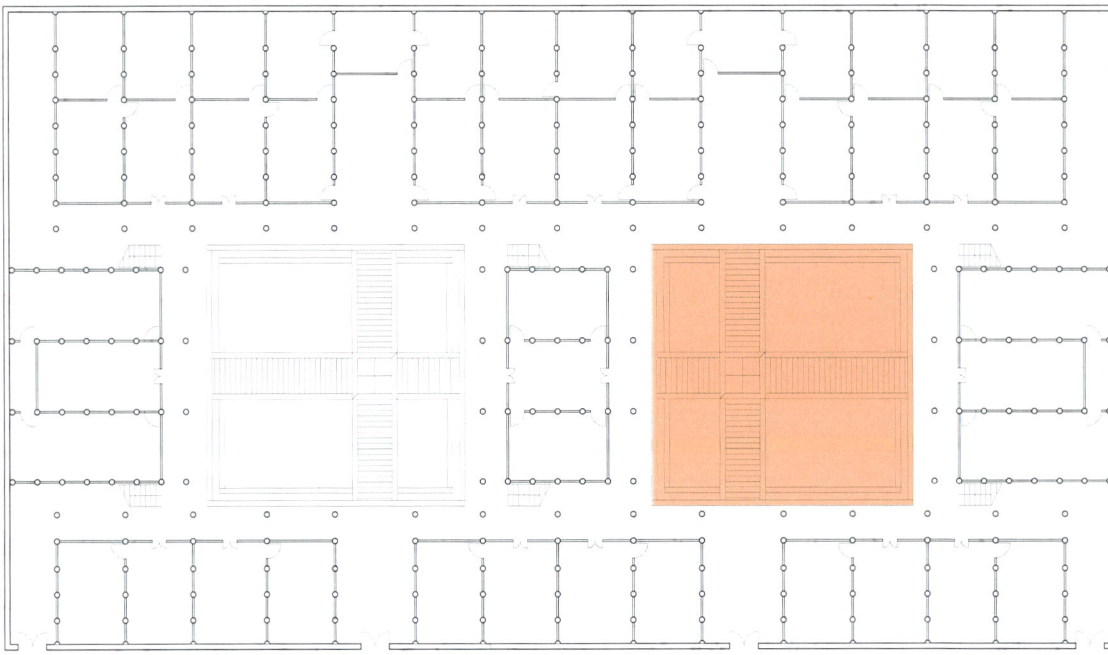

Courtyard for Tea
Roasting and Sundry

About the Author

Zhouhan Li is an architect with a deep interest in the intersection of architecture, trade, and social relations. After earning her undergraduate degree in architecture from Nanjing University, China, Zhouhan pursued an M.Arch at Cornell University, completing the program in December 2023.

Her academic journey has been marked by a keen focus on architectural anthropology, particularly through her involvement in rural workshops during her study in Nanjing University. These experiences allowed her to engage with village communities in China, exploring how urban and architectural formations are intertwined with trade and social dynamics.

Her undergraduate thesis, "Modern Shaping of the Tea Industrial Landscape in Foochow Port in the Perspective of Maritime Tea Trade," reflects this interest at the urban scale. This research was further deepened by the Hart Howerton Travel and Research Fellowship in 2023, through which she extended her exploration of tea trade into the architectural scale. This culminated in a graduate thesis that focused on the restoration and renovation of a specific tea-trade community in Fuzhou, China, aiming to revitalize it for contemporary tea-related activities.

Zhouhan is passionate about using her research to inform practical design solutions that resonate with historical contexts while meeting modern needs. Her work continues to explore how architecture can bridge the past and present, creating spaces that are both meaningful and functional.

The Unseen Buildings of the Internet

Patrick Sardo

Fig. A
Section chunk of a speculative future design for a human-less data center.

The Data Center is possibly the most important building typology of our time, while also being mostly unknown to the public. Data centers are the most visible form of the Internet's physical infrastructure, storing and transmitting data for social media, email, e-commerce platforms, artificial intelligence tools, file storage, and anything else connected online. Anyone with Internet access uses these buildings every day without knowing where they are, what they do, and how important they are to the way we live. The future of this architectural typology is uncertain as society continues to become more aware of issues around big-tech surveillance, climate change, and urban-rural planning practices. The data center is at the core of debates around these issues, while the average person may not even realize they exist. In my graduate thesis, "Posthuman Architectures: Buildings Without Humans", the data center is one of four architectural typologies that is rapidly becoming posthuman as technological advancements in autonomous robotics, artificial intelligence, and data interconnectivity change our relationship to buildings we are actively and passively using on a regular basis.

The foundation of the Internet as we know it today was started partly as a military invention, where high-speed telecommunications was seen as an important tool in the Cold War against the Soviet Union (Ruthfield 1995; NSF 2008). From the 1960s to

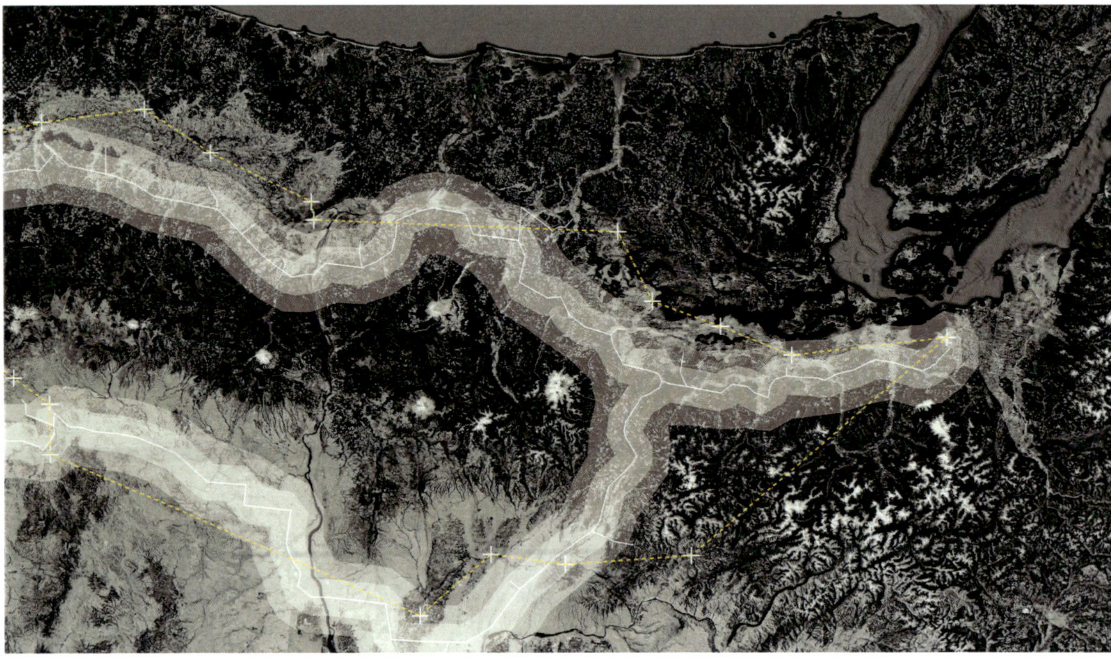

Fig. B
Continuous physical network of underground data centers between metropolitan areas.

the 1980s, U.S. military funding accelerated the development of ARPANET, while other public and private networks continued to grow in complexity and size. Eventually, these networks would be merged into the modern internet that we continue to use today (Leiner et al. 2023). As the networks between government agencies, universities, and private institutions developed, the at-large public benefit of globally interconnected digital networks was undeniable, but no one could have predicted the scale of growth seen in the 1990s and beyond.

Northern Virginia and Washington D.C. would become the center of the major government-funded networks because of their proximity to national defense agencies. This area continued to be a hotspot for the continuously growing World Wide Web as its use skyrocketed in the late 1980s and 1990s. North of Dulles Airport, 40 minutes outside Washington D.C., several hundred data centers are interspersed between shopping centers and residential subdivisions. Loudon County and Prince William County host an ever-growing number of data centers, using tens of millions of square feet of floor area dedicated to server space and pulling thousands of megawatts of energy from the power grid (Miller 2023). This industry has significant political and economic influence locally and nationally, often to the dismay of nearby

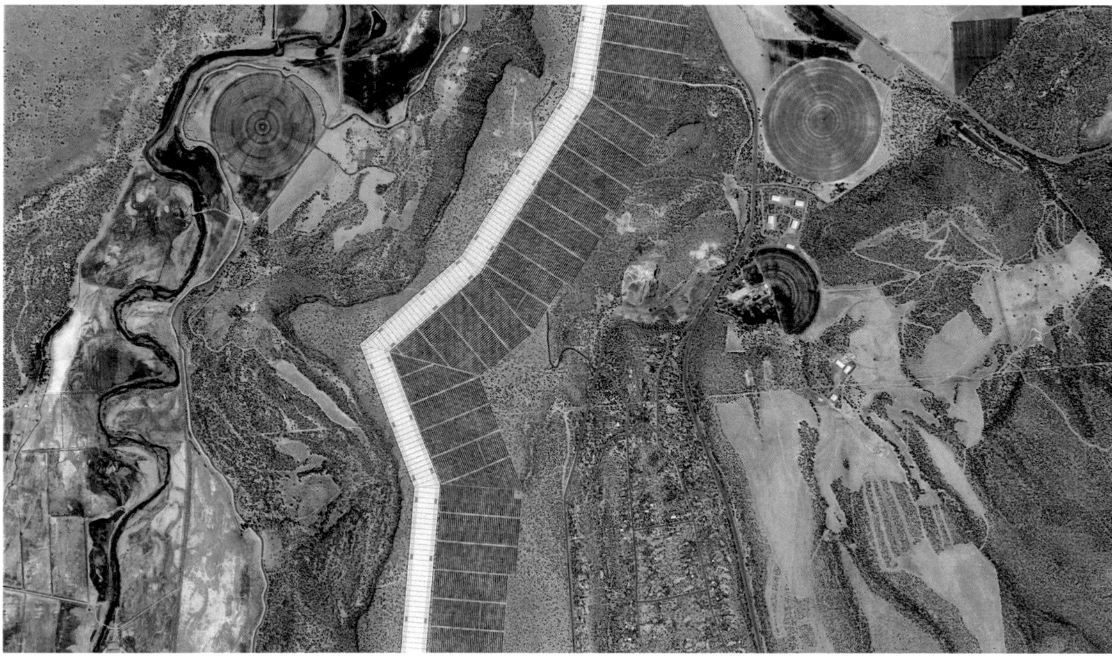

Fig. C
Aerial plan detail of the 500-foot-wide continuous data center and solar farm array.

homes and businesses. Corporations,including Amazon Web Services, Google, Microsoft, and others, are constantly building new facilities across the country and the rest of the world to expand their network and meet the needs of an industry that is continuously growing rapidly year after year (Bangalore et al. 2023).

Data centers operate in contemporary society as the most everyday form of architecture. Every citizen of the digital world uses them, rarely thinking about how their data is transmitted or stored. The proliferation of data storage existing as a "cloud" has rendered the data center invisible to most, while its physical presence is silently creeping into the suburban fabric of most cities. Some regions have much higher concentrations of these buildings for economic, environmental, and political reasons. Politicians and private companies may offer tax incentives, easier and cheaper access to energy and water, and zoning or code variances to bring companies into the area. To better serve internet users, it is better to site data centers near large metropolitan areas. Data centers were initially relegated to the fringes of the exurban rings of cities, part of what Keller Easterling describes as infrastructure space, the "soupy matrix of details and repeatable formulas that generate most of the space in the world" (Easterling 2016). Cheap and underutilized farmland far outside of the suburban sprawl became ideal locations for warehouses until the sprawl continued to expand as cities continued to grow. In a speculative future, the data center may become a continuous network of servers moving across the landscape above and below ground. The previously unseen digital infrastructure network would become more visible as internet use and demand continue to rapidly grow.

The increase in users and content of the internet and data cloud services requires complicated and extensive physical infrastructure for power, cooling, server storage, and transmission lines. When browsing the internet, sending emails and files, and backing up storage drives, a massive network of unseen physical infrastructure is humming away to ensure people can be digitally connected. At a moment's notice, a user's stored data is rapidly sent from a server to a phone, computer, or other connected device, while outside, massive air conditioning units send in cooling air to each server, consuming as much energy as a small town. Corporations that provide data storage and transmission services advertise the illusion that the internet is an amorphous thing, a "cloud", but are conveniently quiet about the immense amounts of energy and water used to maintain the digital illusion. Some data center companies have started building off-site solar farms to offset their considerable energy use, often to alleviate pressure from local governments and energy providers. In the near future, every new data center or part of a continuous network of physical data centers may have on-site renewable energy production.

Architectural design is far less important in the process of creating the physical infrastructure for the digital world. The process of getting a data center built requires more time spent on dealing with zoning variances and political or economic incentives compared to architectural design. Systems engineers designing the server infrastructure inside the outer shell of the building drive the architectural decisions. Data centers are purely functional, and their appearance is often very repetitive even between different regions, architects, and clients. The architect is a formality in the process, only providing the bare minimum of services and a stamp of approval to construct a building that has already been designed through a template.

These buildings are mostly anonymous aesthetically and architecturally, with gray and beige precast concrete panels and the occasional glass storefront, yet rarely any signage or branding. Other than barbed wire fences and armed security gates, there is little indication of these buildings' massive importance to our everyday lives. Most data centers are 100,000 - 300,000 square feet, one to three stories tall, with an army of generators and air conditioning units along the sides to ensure everything inside runs smoothly. Inside, a steel structural frame allows wide open floor plans filled with racks of server computers filled with high-speed storage drives. Human workers are few and far between, as once the construction is finished, only a small team of people work inside, slowly adding servers and ramping up the building's capacity over time. Day-to-day operations at a running data center only require several onsite workers to perform maintenance, leaving most of the space not designed for human comfort or occupation.

Data centers represent a posthuman building typology that is not oriented toward human occupation but toward human consumption and maximum efficiency. Our formal understanding of architecture as a tool or a profession starts to fundamentally change when humans are no longer the active users or occupiers of buildings, alienating all people from the production of goods, food, technology, and data. What was once defined as architecture becomes infrastructure, rarely seen or heard by the public but constantly running in the background to provide a necessary service. Data centers could become completely automated, as robots and other intelligent non-human machines perform tasks that have traditionally been performed by human laborers. This change will remove many constraints on architects and systems engineers, such as fire codes and occupancy, making buildings denser and more efficient.

The shift towards human-less buildings in the future will create unprecedented challenges for architects and designers. Our typical understanding of architectural design breaks down in places like data centers, where decisions are no longer made based on improving or elevating human experience, or even referencing the human as a metric for design in the first place. It is one of the few building types in the world that is already very close to becoming human-less, as the internal processes are relatively simple and easy to maintain. Architects, engineers, and other designers must adapt their past experiences to design new forms of building that operate at different scales with new layouts, sites, materiality, interior climatic conditions, and technology. "Posthuman Architectures: Buildings Without Humans" proposes a speculative future design for a massive infrastructural-scale data center that is continuous both above and below ground. While the project is informed by current design methodologies and growing trends in the industry, the future of the data center remains uncertain.

Fig. D
Collage of below- to above-ground transition of the future data center.

References:

Bangalore, Srini, Arjita Bhan, Andrea Del Miglio, Pankaj Sachdeva, Vijay Sarma, Raman Sharma, and Bhargs Srivathsan. "Investing in the Rising Data Center Economy." McKinsey & Company. January 17, 2023. https://www.mckinsey.com/industries/technology-media-and-telecommunications/our-insights/investing-in-the-rising-data-center-economy.

Easterling, Keller. *Extrastatecraft: The Power of Infrastructure Space* (London: Verso, 2016), 11.

Leiner, Barry M., Vinton G. Cerf, David D. Clark, Robert E. Kahn, Leonard Kleinrock, Daniel C. Lynch, Jon Postel, Larry G. Roberts, and Stephen Wolff. "A Brief History of the Internet." Internet Society. October 11, 2023. https://www.internetsociety.org/internet/history-internet/brief-history-internet/.

Miller, Rich. "Dominion: Virginia's Data Center Cluster Could Double in Size." Data Center Frontier. October 11, 2023. https://www.datacenterfrontier.com/energy/article/33013010/dominion-virginias-data-center-cluster-could-double-in-size.

"NSF and the Birth of the Internet - Special Report: NSF - National Science Foundation." U.S. National Science Foundation. Date updated: April 29, 2008. https://www.nsf.gov/news/special_reports/nsf-net/textonly/60s.jsp.

Ruthfield, Scott. "The Internet's History and Development: From Wartime Tool to the Fish-Cam." In *XRDS: Crossroads, The ACM Magazine for Students, Special Issue on Networks*, September 1, 1995. https://dl.acm.org/doi/fullHtml/10.1145/332198.332202.

Fig. E
Partial section detail of human-less data center.

About the Author

Patrick Sardo is a designer in Boston and holds a Master of Architecture from University of Virginia and an undergraduate degree in architecture from the Knowlton School of Architecture at Ohio State University. Sardo has worked with Bruner/Cott, KUTONOTUK, Arctic Design Group, and Charlottesville Zoning Design Workshop. His research focuses on automated fulfillment centers, data centers, and other architectural typologies emerging from the digital industrial revolution.

Foolishness

Philip Edmonston

Foolishness is the reacquaintance with the experience of one's body in space. Foolishness, the power to step outside the constraints of rationality and into a space of suspended disbelief, opens a multiplicity of interpretations, enabling a person to derive delight from beauty. This power appears to the rational citizen to be foolish — how could anything be beyond explanation? Truly it is only through this foolishness that a more intimate understanding can be found, beyond architectural logic and beyond immediate explanation. It is foolishness that engages with the delight of a too-narrow alley, a shadowy room, and a creaky window.

Foolishness responds to the tension brought up by Bernard Tschumi in *The Pleasure of Architecture* between useful and useless design. Tschumi argues that the pressure to conform to a singular programmatic function (to make ultimately useful space), is set against the architect's imperative to design how she best sees fit (potentially creating space that does not serve one function alone) (Tschumi 1994). If uselessness is the antithesis of functionality and efficiency, what motivates architects to create useless space? Tschumi defends uselessness in Parc de La Villette through his thirty-five Folies, arguing that useless space provides an unrestrictive frame for human activity, which brings meaning to architectural work. He claims that as purely compositional features, the Folies repel function or interpretation, as they neither bear relation to formal logics of historic garden follies nor suggest any single, permanent use. Because of their intentional lack of clear meaning, Tschumi argues that Folies represent architecture in its purest form: because the Folies are a complete break from convention, they are the perfect unrestrictive frame for events, and the perfect defense of uselessness (Derrida 1986).

Fig. B
Diagram "Site, Intervention, Water"

While the project provides a fascinating argument against architecture centering function alone, Parc de La Villette has been criticized because it focuses solely on Tschumi's intellectual project, and not on the human experience of the work of design. This focus is made clear in how the project's development begins with a cartesian point grid and is further shown in how Tschumi communicates the ideas behind the project — not through the Parc itself, but rather through complex formal diagrams depicting the manipulations of grids, independent of site (Jones 2012). The Parc and its Folies, because they are designed with respect to ideal notions and not to actual experiential qualities, are not made for humans. The Parc has value as a theoretical project, but it seems incomplete as a work of architecture because of its negligence of how it will affect those who experience it.

While Tschumi's work considers uselessness as a goal, Carlo Scarpa's Palazzo Querini Stampalia is useless only when it seeks to evoke wonder in those who experience it. While most of the project is useful as circulation and exhibit space, half of the porch of the palazzo is below water level, and cannot be used in any practical way by visitors. Of the precious Venetian square footage, Scarpa did the unthinkable, giving half of a room's floor space to the canal — a clever physical involvement of context, an exquisite spatial move, but a functionally useless one (Zambonini 1983). While only half of the room is useful, the water's imposition on the interior of the building evokes delight in its strangeness, and in the way it situates the subject in a distinctly Venetian space. Scarpa's work is not isolated as Tschumi's is, rather it is a mutation of the Venetian everyday. In his renovation of the palace, Scarpa sought to emphasize the historic palace and its location along the Venetian canal. In referring to both the original building and its unique site, Scarpa's work invites visitors to experience its spatial and historic context anew, while Parc de La Villette, which is intentionally divorced from its context, does not.

Scarpa's interior canal space is evocative precisely because it is useless. Because it is not conventional or functional, the space surprises those who experience it and encourages them to better understand the character of the Palazzo's spatial and historic context. The power of uselessness to evoke delight is clear in our everyday lives, too. It is in mistakes, in moments when things go

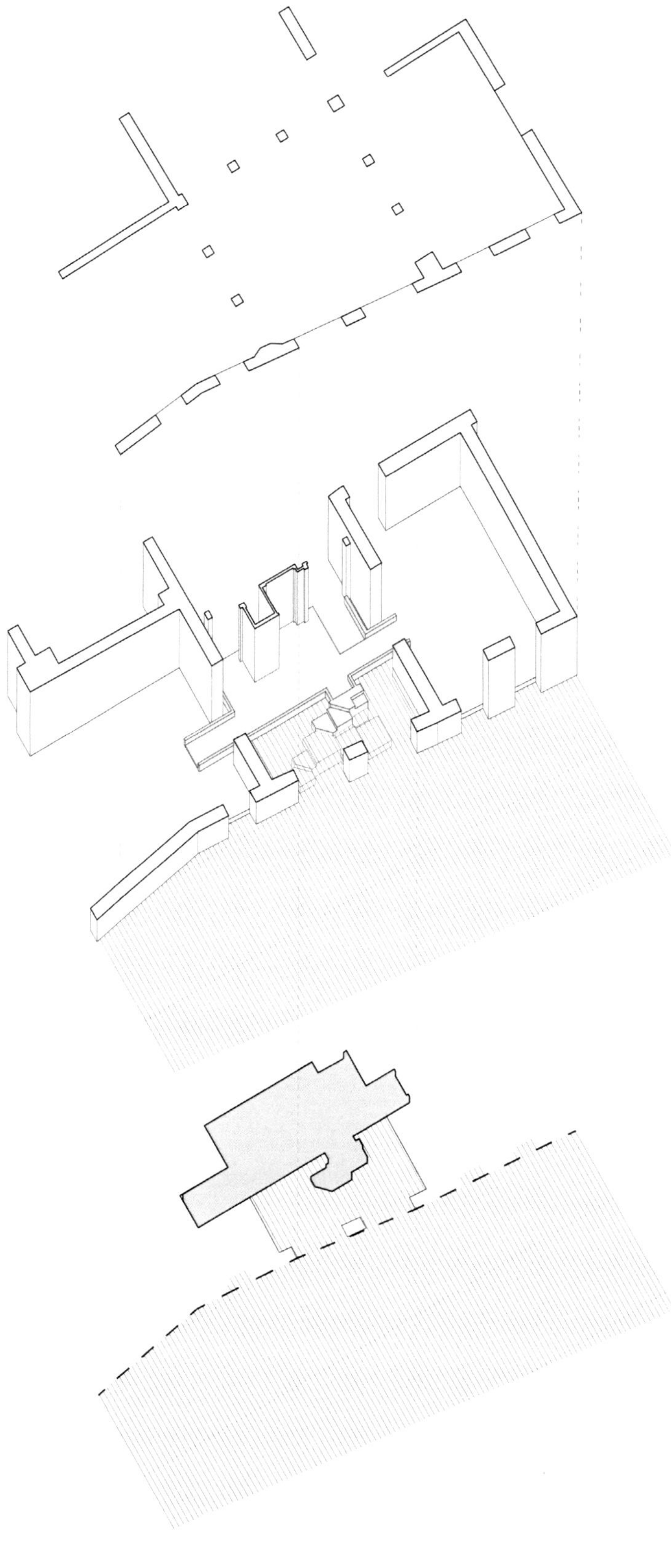

Initial Site Condition

Scarpa's Design

Floor and Water Condition

awry, that we are jolted into the experience of ourselves - from the analytic to the foolish. We might compare Scarpa's work to a common experience: the dropping of a coffee cup. The instance of dropping (and shattering, and spilling), in its violence and inconvenience, breaks the analytic trance. The shattered cup is no longer a container for hot liquid but has mutated. The new form, shards of ceramic, and a splatter of coffee evoke the past form of a coffee cup but do not themselves have the same (or any) use. In the same way, Scarpa transformed half of the palazzo's porch room to be useless, but also to evoke the experience of the palazzo's place in Venice. Instances like the dropping of a cup demand that we experience our bodies in space and remind us of the arbitrariness of everyday "usefulness". It is because of this that one might foolishly delight in dropping a coffee cup.

If a work of architecture insists on uselessness, it must also insist on evocation. The goal of architecture may not be what it is, so much as its power to inspire meaningful experiences in those who visit it. In evoking something ephemeral, like delight, architecture loosens the bonds of "usefulness" and takes flight. Evocation is not a rigid input-output operation, rather it is as its root suggests, a calling forth - an invitation to feel or to act. As shown in Scarpa's Stampalia and the coffee cup, this invitation is inherent in things that push us to reevaluate our experience of the mundane everyday. How can a rational person accept this invitation to delight in architectural moments and spilled coffee? One must step back from convention and experience foolishly.

References:

Derrida, Jacques. "POINT DE FOLIE – MAINTENANT L'ARCHITECTURE. Bernard Tschumi: La Case Vide – La Villette, 1985." *AA Files*, no. 12 (1986): 65–75. http://www.jstor.org/stable/29543519.

Jones, Peter Blundell. "Parc de La Villette in Paris, France, by Bernard Tschumi." *Architectural Review*, June 7, 2012. https://www.architectural-review.com/buildings/parc-de-la-villette-in-paris-france-by-bernard-tschumi.

Tschumi, Bernard. "The Pleasure of Architecture." In *Architecture and Disjunction* (Cambridge, MA: MIT Press, 1994), 173 – 183.

Zambonini, Giuseppe. "Process and Theme in the Work of Carlo Scarpa." *Perspecta* 20 (1983): 21–42. https://doi.org/10.2307/1567064.

About the Author

Philip Edmonston is a fourth year Pre-Professional Architecture student from South Jersey. He is currently working on his undergraduate thesis with Peter Waldman, which focuses on reusing an industrial site in Camden, New Jersey as a neighborhood center. In his free time, he loves sketching, reading, and cooking.

Questioning

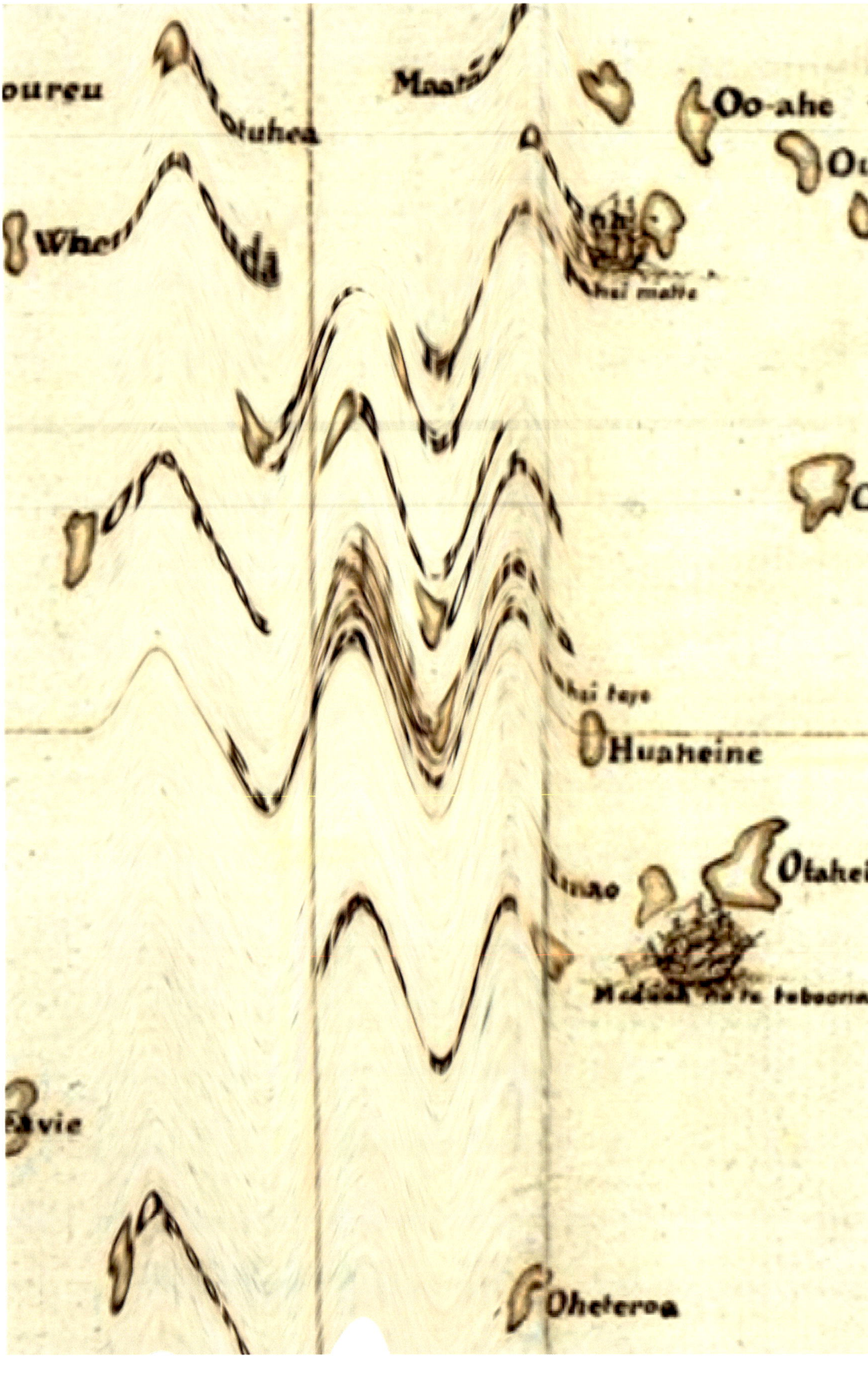
oureu
Oo-ahe
Huaheine
Oheteroa

‘E avatea

Translation as design process

Sean Kois

> *“It matters what thoughts think thoughts. It matters what knowledges know knowledges. It matters what relations relate relations. It matters what worlds world worlds. It matters what stories tell stories.”*
>
> *– Donna J. Haraway in Staying with the Trouble: Making Kin in the Chthulucene (2016, p. 35)*

Introduction

In the convention of our customary Gregorian calendar, July 1769 marks the beginning of a momentous encounter between two vastly different, and uniquely opposed, human worldviews. Tupaia, a native of the land contemporarily known as the Society Islands, a priest of the ‘Oro religion, member of the arioi cult, master navigator, and advisor to the chiefs of Tahiti would serendipitously cross paths with Captain James Cook during his lauded expedition, sailing the Endeavour throughout the South Seas. Cook, an Englishman sent by the Crown on his first of three eventual voyages, was charged with observing and recording the 1769 transit of Venus across the Sun for the advancement of European science, as well as to explore and document the distant ocean and the fabled Terra Australis. Tupaia, well-respected and influential in his own world, would eventually be recognized as a valuable addition to the Europeans’ exploration and would be asked to join the captain as an interpreter and navigator of the vast Pacific Ocean (Salmond 2005).

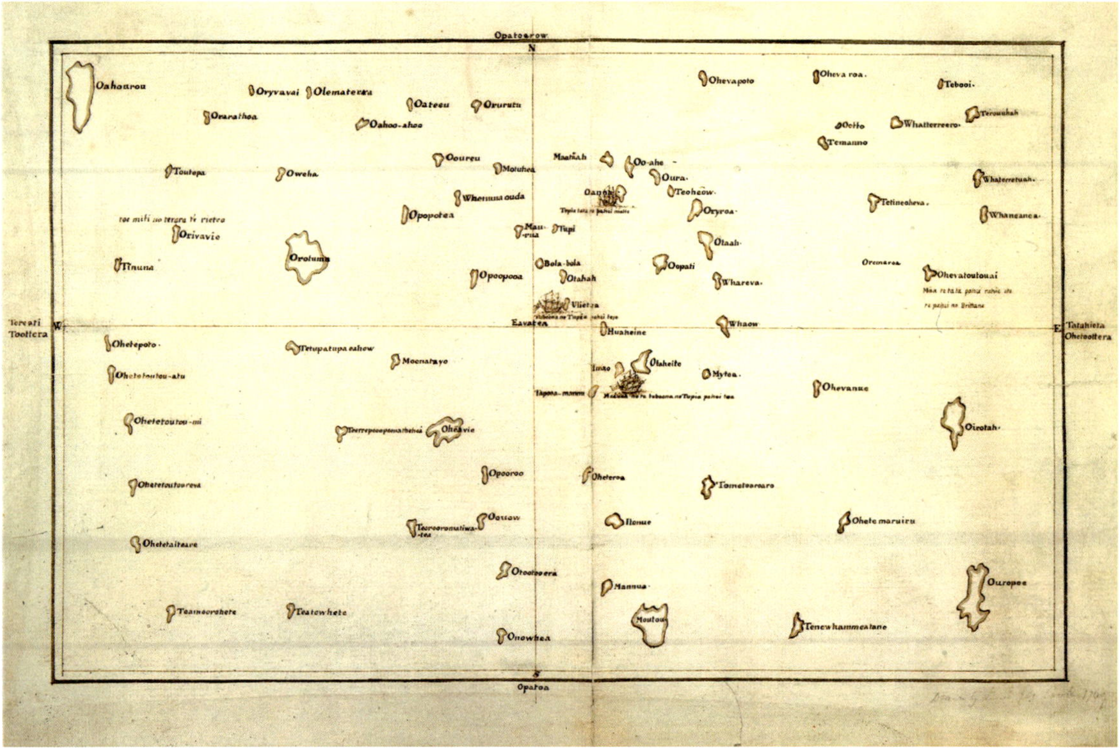

By this time, of course, the European colonialists had already explored a significant portion of the globe, leaving a wake of disease, erasure, extraction, and revisionist historicity, the legacy of which is well documented and rightfully critiqued. Happening notably late in the timeline of European exploration, this was certainly not the first occasion an indigenous navigator had bolstered a European exploration, nor did it end much differently than one might expect. After only 18 months of sailing, Tupaia would die unceremoniously from illness in Batavia, in the Dutch East Indies — what is now present day Jakarta, Indonesia. During their brief time together, however, Cook and Tupaia would collaborate on a set of cartographic drawings of immense, if not obfuscated, value to global history. These drawings would remain mostly unknown for centuries and have only recently come to light as being an incredible feat of cross-cultural communication — a specific act of mapping as, or of, translation that has an important reverberance for the fields of architecture and spatial design.

Fig. A
Tupaia's Map, 1770.

Having long been cryptic and misunderstood due to the odd spatial arrangement of defined islands, these maps have been mostly ignored by researchers and, at best, considered an enigma. If we consider the final version of the set, commonly referred to as "Tupaia's Map" (Fig. A) through the reasoning of a Eurocentric Mercator map projection, the confusion caused by poorly translated and transcribed island names is compounded by the fact that any identifiable islands are so far out of position and scale, in relation to one another, that the drawing is nearly incomprehensible. On initial inspection, most people could likely identify "Bola-bola" on the drawing as Bora-bora and recognize it as being appropriately drawn in relation to "Otaheite", known currently as Tahiti. However, while "Orotuma", or current day Rotuma, is vaguely drawn in an appropriate direction from the other two islands, it is drawn wildly out of scale in both size and distance. In reality, it's a similar size to Bora-bora, at about thirteen times the distance, and at a slightly more northern bearing. This example is one of many incongruencies that was certainly in mind when Cook and others discredited the maps, and shelved them for posterity.

Now, new understandings of the map have been outlined in a recently published article by Lars Eckstein and Anja Schwarz, titled "The Making of Tupaia's Map: A Story of the Extent and Mastery of Polynesian Navigation, Competing Systems of Wayfinding on James Cook's Endeavour, and the Invention of an Ingenious Cartographic System." In this peer-reviewed article the authors, in conversation with other published works, are describing recent developments in how their research is advancing new insights about these drawings as a novel form of navigational cartography, which they call the "avatea system." This emergent body of inquiry is beginning to make sense of Tupaia's maps, suggesting that, rather than being some sort of representation of the miscalculation or misunderstanding of an uneducated Polynesian, these drawings are very concretely an exercise in translation.

> *"Tupaia's Map is one of the most famous and enigmatic artefacts to emerge from the early encounters between Europeans and Pacific Islanders... The chart not only underscores the extent and mastery of Polynesian navigation, it is also a remarkable feat of translation between two very different wayfinding systems and their respective representational models."*
> *— (Eckstein and Schwarz 2019, Abstract)*

Instrument

It won't be shocking to highlight that the work of translating doesn't seem to have been equitably shared by the two parties, and that many original records, including the drawings, are riddled with questions and skepticism from the European explorers. By all accounts however, Tupaia was welcome and actively worked with Cook and certain members of the ship's crew at the large work table inside the great cabin of the Endeavour. Turnbull notes, "At any one time there could have been as many as 11 men of all classes and rankings at the table working on their special tasks. The men involved in the collaborative drawing of the chart at various times included the captain, master, mate and a seaman, all Royal Navy personnel of differing ranks with a wide range of capacities in navigation, calculation, mapmaking, drawing and ship handling" (Turnbull 2019). Among them, and at the right hand of the captain, was the ship master Robert Molyneux, who recorded a list of 130 island names in the ship's log, some of which were congruent with islands known to the Europeans, and all of which likely came from the reciting of navigational chants by the master navigator, Tupaia.

Herein lies the first of two key points, both pivotal in understanding the avatea system: a list of island names, recorded by European hand, in an order resembling a sequence of oral recollection, common to the traditions of Polynesian wayfinding. We cannot know for certain if these specific sequences were part of the oral tradition or not, though Molyneux himself comments in his journal on the assuredness of Tupaia in reciting the island sequences, and it remains a central claim of Eckstein and Schwarz. The diagrammatic interpretation of Eckstein and Schwarz's sequences on a contemporary Mercator projection of the Pacific highlights the breadth Tupaia's navigational knowledge (Fig. B).

> *"Sequences, we argue below, are indispensable for understanding Tupaia's Map, which does not depict an ocean abstracted from the traveller but invites viewers to follow distinct voyaging itineraries through the sea of islands."*
> *— (Eckstein and Schwarz 2019, pg. 18)*

Of specific interest, and the second key to understanding this translation, is the term "'E avatea" being written at the center of each of the three remaining versions of the map. The most straightforward translation of this term from Tupaia's native Polynesian language is "at noon." Eckstein and Schwarz posit that the representational designation of avatea is a direct result of Tupaia observing the importance and daily measure of the noon sun by his European counterparts. Whereas the measure of the sun at midday in Polynesian navigational systems was relatively insignificant, for the Europeans it was absolutely paramount. This observed distinction by Tupaia seems to have become an essential point of translation between the two cultures, and while there were undoubtedly easily imagined scenarios of language and normative cultural exchange to be decoded interpersonally, it is my view that this precise exercise of translation, by nature requiring a compromise in understanding between worldviews, is an exciting example of how fieldwork and co-mapping for spatial design may potentially be diagrammed and implemented in contemporary circumstances.

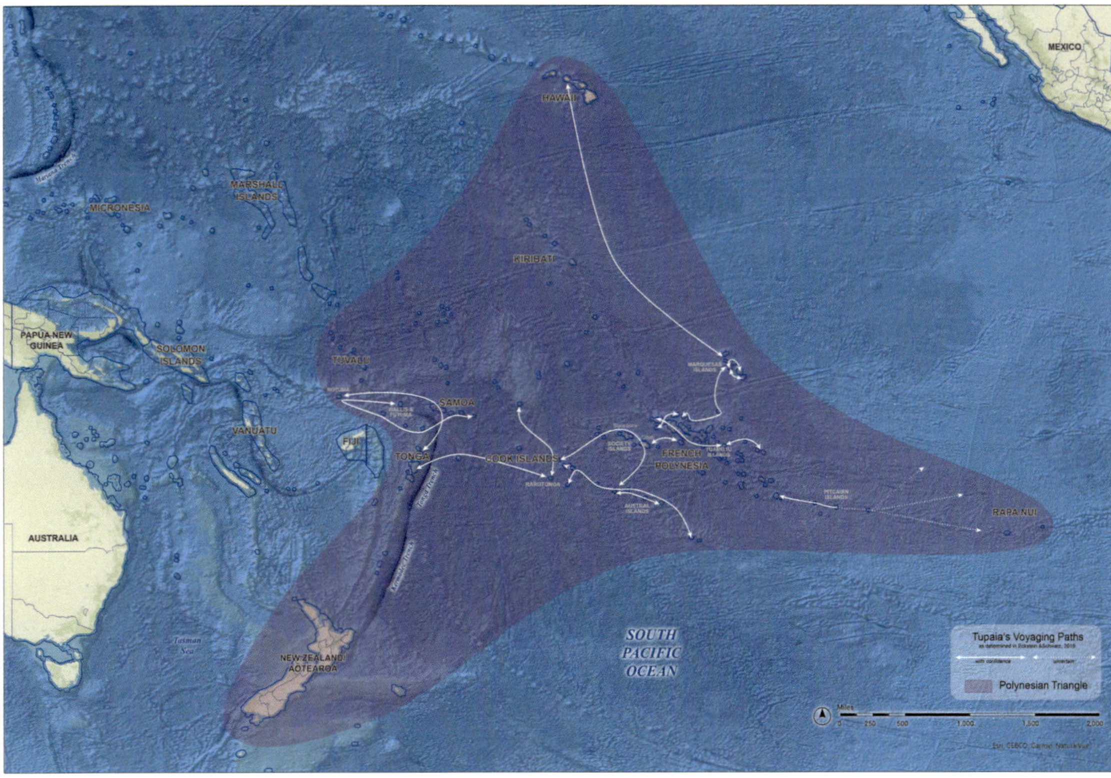

Fig. B
A diagram of Tupaia's voyaging paths, as outlined by Eckstein and Schwarz.

Principally drawn by Tupaia, the mappings can be understood, not as a measured drawing projecting through a cartesian grid, but rather as an assemblage of sequences, understood through the lens of a Polynesian wayfinder and expanded from a measured point, through the lens of European navigators. While island size and planimetric shape are important for European cadastral understandings, they are all but irrelevant for Polynesian open-ocean navigation, and so rightly neglected in Tupaia's drawings, much to the frustration of Cook and researchers hence.

To explain its use succinctly let's clarify that Tupaia's avatea system, as described by Eckstein and Schwarz, denotes the western cardinal direction of north by the term 'E avatea, and places it at the center of the map; an accurate transmutation of the fact that in the southern hemisphere the sun at noon lies in a northern bearing. From there, intrepid avatea navigators would draw a bearing line from the center of the map to the island from which they are starting their voyage and draw another bearing line from their starting island to their destination. Measured in a clockwise direction, the bearing reading from the first line to the second, respectively, would be the appropriate heading for navigation.

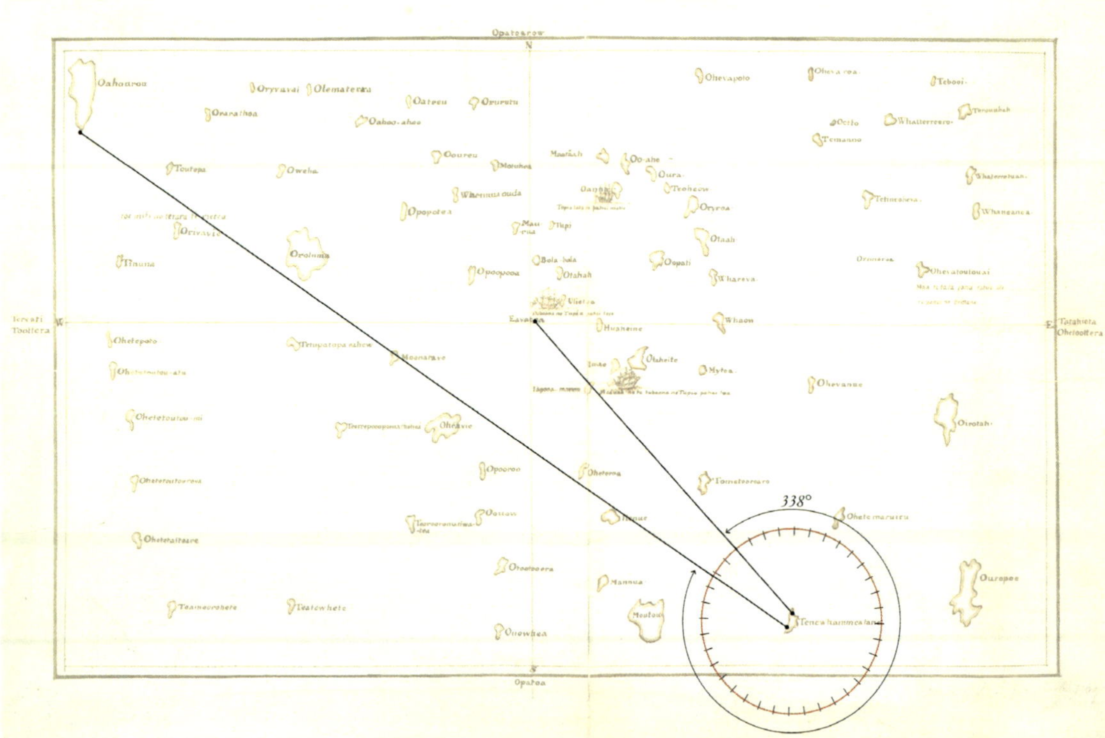

Fig. C
A diagram of the navigational bearing from the Marquesas Islands to O'ahu in the avatea system, as outlined by Eckstein & Schwarz.

Eckstein and Schwarz provide a stunning example of how accurate the system is by taking a measurement of one of the longest sequences, from the Marquesas Islands group to O'ahu in Hawai'ian chain, a distance spanning nearly 2,500 miles. Measured on the most prominent existing version of Tupaia's map (Fig. C), the bearing between the Marquesas, labeled "Tenewhammaetane", and O'ahu, labeled "Oahourou", is approximately 338°. It is approximately 335° on an earlier version of the map. The actual bearing, measured on a contemporary Mercator map projection (Fig. D) is 330° NNW. It should be noted that I did take some liberties to ensure the diagrams (Figs C+D) would match the accounting and measurements of Eckstein and Schwarz. However, the accuracy of the system being measured on old maps that have been drawn and redrawn by multiple hands, using representations of large archipelagos as single units, and the consistency with which it can be proven relative to contemporary mapping practices, is nothing short of astounding.

Importance

The resilience and ingenuity of Polynesian culture cannot be overstated. Their legacy is rich with mythic origin stories, seafaring wayfinders, and stout survival in the face of an often harsh, unforgiving environment. Battered by seasonal cyclones,

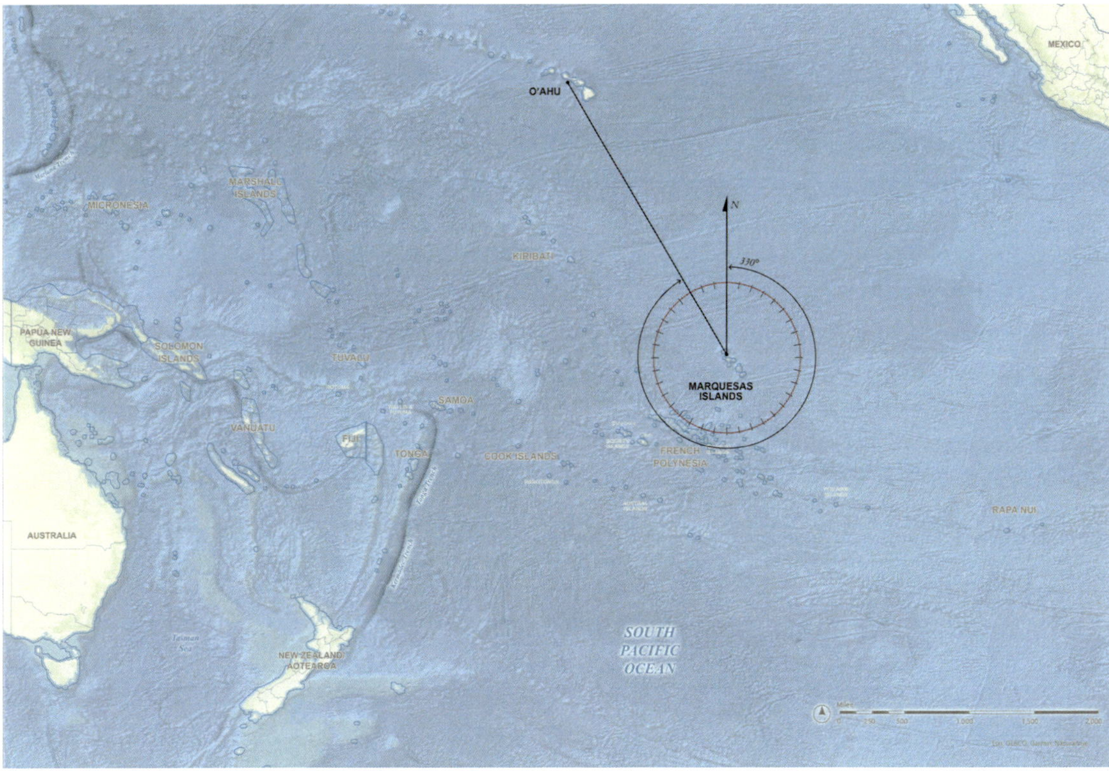

Fig. D
A diagram of the navigational bearing from the Marquesas Islands to O'ahu in the contemporary Mercator map projection.

scorched by equatorial sun, limited by land mass, and resigned to challenging fishing and food storage techniques, the story of Polynesia is the story of a people determined to remain. In the face of the modern and ever-growing problems of climate change, how are the cultural landscapes and architecture of these Pacific Peoples to assure their own identity and longevity into the twenty-first century? What challenges are hardest and most important to them? What lessons can the design professions learn from their history, their historical and modern building techniques, and the way their spatial organization defines their relationships to one another and to their environment?

I believe that an investigation into these questions will lead us to a more complete picture of the global human condition, and how best to understand and engage with it. Recognizing the architecture of Polynesian longhouses may give us insight into their physical structure and how it operates under cyclone wind loads, but also how it operates as a social organizer while being constructed and inhabited. Lithograph prints from the Pacific expedition of Captain Dumont d'Urville (Figs E+F) show us snapshots of the inanimate materiality of traditional building techniques, imbued with the social characteristics of both intimate, at-home life as well as a more public, ceremonial gathering. While artistic liberties, and the

Fig. E.
Lithograph of an interior view of a traditional Tongan house (fale).

translation of the moment into an image, should certainly be taken into account, these images stand in stark contrast to photographs of contemporary Tongan houses (Fig. G). Something as mundane as woven coconut fiber sennit (lalava in Tongan), used as lashing in traditional construction techniques, may provide us insight into how people relate to the material origins of their structures beyond merely their organic beginnings. In his Master of Architecture thesis, Latu notes that "[i]nvestigating the metaphorical meaning behind lalava showcases its versatility as an art form and constructional method – not separating the two contexts but embracing both as one" (Latu 2022).

These understandings will allow architects and landscape architects to design environments and spaces more completely. A focused inquiry into these spatial topics can lead, not to a set of specific design propositions but rather to a sort of framework for understanding, within architecture, as well as a critique of existing practice. Importantly, I believe it's not the place of western designers to define or prescribe specific spatial design propositions, lest not without any sort of direct collaboration with interested counterparts or stakeholders. "Architecture" as a field has been woefully inadequate in fulfilling its contemporary promise of culturally sensitive practice while simultaneously espousing the

Fig. F.
Lithograph of a traditional kava ceremony.

universality of western spatial constructs, underpinned by superficial social and cultural analysis. While architectural history and theory courses are often sufficient in surveying historic, popular, and contemporary modes of western European design fanaticism, they are insufficient with respect to a rigorous contemplation of any non-Eurocentric modes of worldbuilding. I use the term "worldbuilding" here specifically in reference and deference to the oft-unified vision of Architecture as a field of the invention and re-invention of idea visualization, building techniques, and spatial understandings; Architecture builds worlds. In as much as we can believe this paramount fact of our field, how then can we justify its cursory and superficial inclusion of traditional, non-western worldview practices?

I will offer personal experience and understandings stemming from my time as a United States Peace Corps volunteer in the Kingdom of Tonga. A particular set of three realizations has long stood out to me, which I will describe here as a simple introduction to my own interest in the subject. First, I came to learn that many Polynesian origin narratives revolve around the demi-god Maui and his travels through the Pacific. As one story goes, Maui, fishing with his mortal brothers along the way, casts his line far out into the ocean, hoping to catch the largest fish of them all. Rather than

Fig. G
A contemporary Tongan fale.

hooking a fish, Maui hooks the ocean floor, and with his legendary might, pulls the land up, out of the water, and thus the islands of Polynesia are born. While this origin narrative, simplified though it may be presented here, is beautiful and poetic in many ways, it also importantly complements two more significant additional cultural facts from the region.

The second understanding to highlight here is the knowledge that Polynesian Wayfinders operate and navigate through the spaces of the Pacific Ocean with the conceptualization that, rather than moving as independent entities through the world-space, they are fixed in position, and moving the world-space around them, calling their destinations into being.

> *"We understand that Oceanic navigation did not abstract the world from the navigator and did not fix it from an abstract exterior focal point of orientation. On the contrary, the geographic centre of navigational orientation was inevitably the navigator, and the pahi, the voyaging canoe (in Society Islander terms), which was imagined as fixed, surrounded by an animate world of ocean, sea life, wind, current, sun, stars, planets, and ultimately islands."*
> *— (Eckstein and Schwarz 2019, pg. 30)*

We can see then that the Polynesian worldview, at least in the sense of traveling through space, is not only completely opposite to that of western Europeans, but that it also closely mirrors the structure of some formative Polynesian origin narratives; Whereas Maui pulled the pacific islands into reality with his fishhook, Wayfinders likewise summon their destinations into tangible reality, as they move the world to themselves.

My third and final realization is an interesting linguistic Tongan turn of phrase. As is Tongan custom, I would always greet and be greeted by others on my frequent walks from my small house into the main town during my time in the country. "Te ke alu ki fe?" ("Where are you going?") I would always be asked. "Te u luelue atu ki kolo!" ("I am walking to town!"), I would respond. Although I was confident in my grammar, having spent months in language training and time at site, I began to realize over and over that Tongans would respond to the same question quite differently. "Te u luelue mai ki kolo," they would say; a subtle, yet very important difference.

In the Tongan language, the adverbs "atu" and "mai" are opposites. Though they don't have any one-to-one translation to English, their sentiment can be described thusly: "atu" signifies "to go away from oneself," whereas "mai" would signify "to come towards oneself." In effect, this meant that in my attempt to translate my own action of walking from my house to the town – a strikingly European directional notion, as it turns out — I was wrongly hoping to convey the sense that "I am walking myself to town." In proper Tongan grammar however, the appropriate response would be to use the term "mai" and convey the sense that "I am walking town to myself." The discrepancy is not insignificant and, I postulate, likely a fundamental distinction in how culture, narrative, language, and worldview define the very syntax of our material lives.

If then, the narratives of demigods pulling lands from the ocean share the same cultural impetus as the linguistic semiotics of describing movement through space, how can western architects and designers be equipped to speculate on the possibility of new spatial arrangements within these cultures? In other words, can the tools of cadastral mappings and Mercator projections sufficiently support the development of architectural spatial outcomes in, of, and for cultures with such fundamentally different ontologies? To me, the response to these questions is a resounding "No". Perhaps, however, the designer's skillset of diagramming, as a medium, is well suited to beginning the process of cultural translation. Here I offer a set of diagrams to relate and begin to translate the contrasting ontologies of Polynesian and Western navigational practices. The gridded plane of latitude and longitude allows the

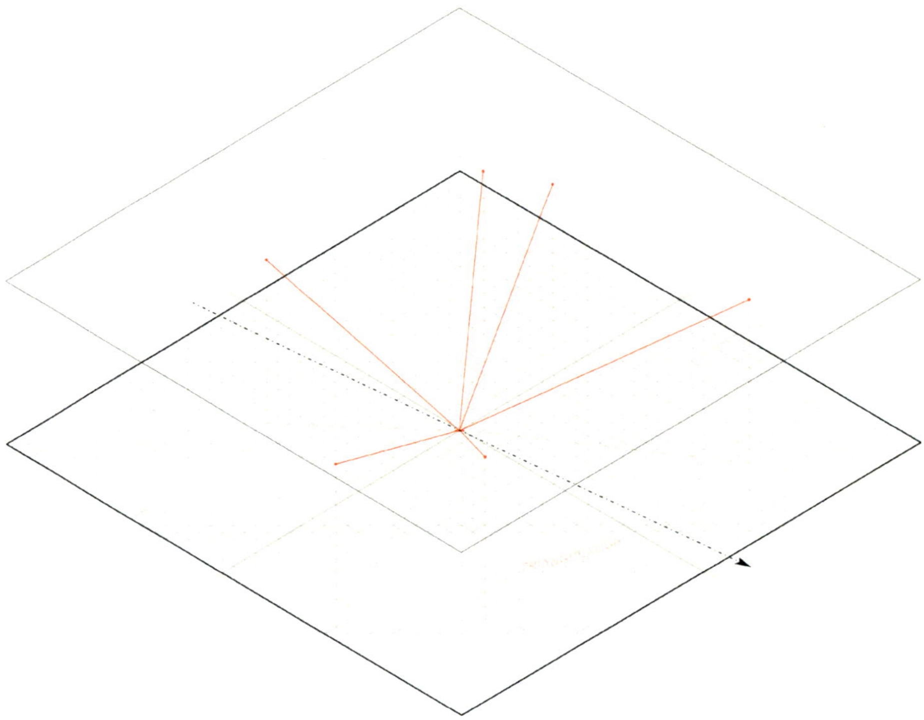

Fig. H
Diagram of Western navigation systems.
Credit: Author

western navigator to triangulate position and heading, codifying the possibility of moving through space into a set of predictable, mathematical outcomes (Fig. H). Polynesian ontology highlights patterns and sequences, coaxing the movement of space around the wayfinder who allows perceptual clues to validate the path of the destination to themselves (Fig. I).

Imperative

At a real and tangible level, architecture and design must move towards a more informed and empathetic mode of work, taking into consideration the immense bodies of research available in the social sciences. We must ask, very concretely, how can design practice work for an equitable future and mitigate erasure of non-western knowledge in the twenty-first century? Are cheap, stick-built, euro-centered design ideas (as pictured in Fig. G) enough? Or are they merely a thinly veiled neo-colonialist tactic, intentional or not, aiding the erosion of the rich cultural fabric of the globe by muting the cultural relevance of spatial worldbuilding? Using the tools of our profession we must gather, understand, and translate existing works from the social sciences, arts, and cross-cultural collaborators to arrive at better and more equitable design propositions for the future.

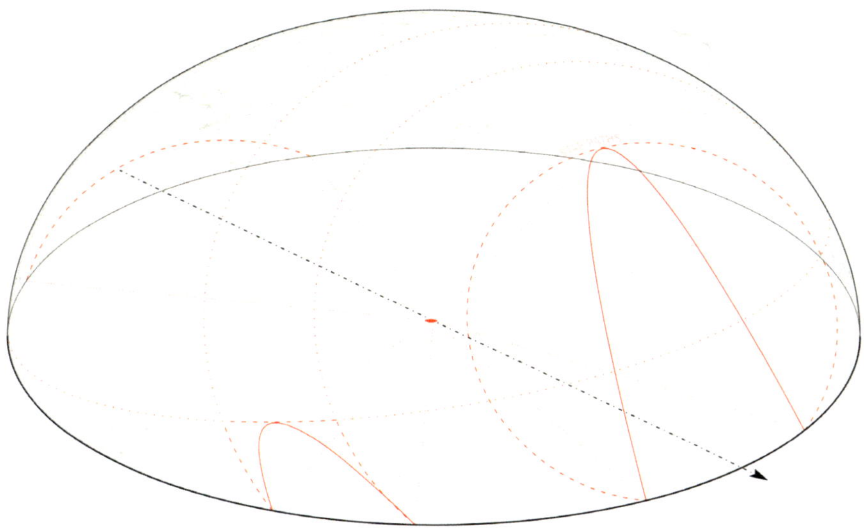

Fig. I
Diagram of Polynesian navigation systems.
Credit: Author

In 2016, Rebuild by Design published their "Elements of Effective Engagement," which defined twelve "best practices" for community engagement, and notably foregrounded a few practices developed by SCAPE for their Living Breakwaters design (Rebuild by Design 2023). This version of community engagement, while certainly a noble and worthwhile commitment, mostly amounts to performative participatory design, and simply increasing legibility of design propositions for public awareness. Actions like "ready-to-mail comment cards" and hosting "combined meetings" are passive collaboration strategies, putting the onus of engagement solely on the community members. Rich, cultural intricacies are rarely, if ever, unveiled by just asking; a depth of understanding can only come from translation. Translation of the mundane, translation of the unspoken, translation of the everyday. Designers must do the work of informing themselves, rather than just asking. Just asking, as the existing practices of community engagement are often carried out, is an extractivist practice. Translation is inherently a coordinated process, often leading to original and genuine outcomes.

Our new methodology should include understanding and diagramming texts from the social sciences and indigenous authors, artists, and cross-cultural collaborators. In her recent publication, *Lo-TEK: Design by Radical Indigenism*, Julia Watson is beginning to do this, albeit at a somewhat superficial level (Watson 2020). Our new methodology should be less like a sort-of artistic representation or analog, and more of a suite of tools for translation and understanding, beyond cartesian mapping and western spatial assumptions. Designers do not have to reinvent how engagement is done; There are fields of research already dedicated to this: Anthropology, Sociology, Cultural History, etc.

As a specific proposition for any cultural landscape, I believe design can produce new, interesting, and appropriate cartographic diagrams and models. These simulacrum may be physical attempts to represent vernacular spatial practices in a manner and method more closely aligned to those vernacular understandings, and in some contrast to currently employed methods in the field of architecture; A translation between two worldviews, not unlike Tupaia's map, that may allow an equitable foothold for both the modes of thought and production.

Images:

Figs A+C: Tupaia's Map, 1770, British Library, London, © British Library Board BL Add MS 21593C

Figs B, D, H, I: Author

Fig. E: General Research Division, The New York Public Library. "Vue intérieure. de la maison des femmes du chef Palou. (Tonga - Tabou.)." The New York Public Library Digital Collections. 1830 - 1835. https://digitalcollections.nypl.org/items/510d47da-78b5-a3d9-e040-e00a18064a99

Fig. F: The New York Public Library Digital Collections. 1830 - 1835. https://digitalcollections.nypl.org/items/510d47da-78ad-a3d9-e040-e00a18064a99

Fig. G: Warner, Chase. "Sheep and Mountains with a Side of Kia Ora: Tonga: Where to Begin...Lol." Sheep and Mountains with a Side of Kia Ora (blog), August 9, 2011. https://rotarychase.blogspot.com/2011/08/tonga-where-to-beginlol.html.

Fig. J: *[A] view of Matavai Bay, [in the island of] Otaheite [Tahiti]*, oil on canvas painting by William Hodges, depicting two ships of Commander James Cook's 2nd expedition to the South Seas, 1776. Royal Museums Greenwich, BHC 1932, Public Domain.

References:

Eckstein, Lars and Anja Schwarz. "The Making of Tupaia's Map: A Story of the Extent and Mastery of Polynesian Navigation, Competing Systems of Wayfinding on James Cook's Endeavour, and the Invention of an Ingenious Cartographic System." *The Journal of Pacific History* 54, no. 1 (2019): 1 – 95. https://doi.org/10.1080/00223344.2018.1512369.

Eckstein, Lars, and Anja Schwarz. "Corrections: An Update to 'The Making of Tupaia's Map.'" *The Journal of Pacific History 58*, no. 1 (2023): 64–80. https://doi.org/10.1080/00223344.2022.2138291.

"Elements of Effective Engagement Report." Rebuild by Design. Accessed July 16, 2023. https://rebuildbydesign.org/uncategorized/elements-of-effective-engagement-report-2/.

Haraway, Donna J. *Staying with the Trouble: Making Kin in the Chthulucene*. Durham, NC: Duke University Press, 2016. https://doi.org/10.2307/j.ctv11cw25q.

Latu, Vena. "Binding Lalava: Unravelling the Functionality of Pattern." Masters Thesis. Auckland University of Technology, 2022. https://hdl.handle.net/10292/15392.

Salmond, Anne. "Their Body Is Different, Our Body Is Different: European and Tahitian Navigators in the 18th Century." *History and Anthropology* 16, no. 2 (2005): 167-186. https://doi.org/10.1080/02757200500116105.

Watson, Julia. *Lo-TEK. Design by Radical Indigenism*. Los Angeles, CA: Taschen America, 2020.

Fig. J
[A] view of Matavai Bay, [in the island of] Otaheite [Tahiti], oil on canvas painting by William Hodges, depicting two ships of Commander James Cook's 2nd expedition to the South Seas, 1776. Public Domain.

About the Author

Sean Kois is a landscape and architectural designer, with a professional background in the construction and landscape trades, as well as being a returned US Peace Corps Volunteer (Tonga, '09 –'13). He holds a bachelor's degree in anthropology, and a dual Master of Architecture and Landscape Architecture, all from UVA. His professional interests are broad, but presently focused on design and implementation of natural and nature-based infrastructure through regional scale methodologies. He is currently an ORISE Research Fellow with the US Army Corps of Engineers, and a Lecturer at the School of Architecture.

Joy

Zlata Onufrieva

While, indeed, "the everyday can appear neutral, mundane or unremarkable", there are fundamental human emotions, such as joy, that are shaped by the consistency, safety and predictability provided by everyday life. The first part of this short film was filmed in 2019, in Moscow, Russia.

Various people were asked to define happiness. The irony of this film lies in that today, the reality and everyday life that shaped their notion of happiness has been shaken by the war initiated by the Russian government against the Ukrainian people and territory.

The second part of the film was completed almost 4 years later, when they were asked to answer the same question. Both the answers and the tone in which they are provided changed dramatically, exhibiting the impact of everyday life into human emotions. While some keep finding joy in new contexts, others are left behind by the bleak environment of contemporary Moscow and refuse to provide an answer.

РАД

Ok, when drunk and dancing I am happy.

ОСТЬ

My reflection in the mirror brings me joy.

Everything was simple.

It brings me joy when I have an easy day.

It brings me joy that I live in a free city.

About the Author

Zlata Onufrieva is a London-based documentary filmmaker with a particular interest in socially conscious stories. Originally from a small city in Siberia, Onufrieva worked as a journalist in Moscow until 2016, when she moved to Prague to study documentary filmmaking at FAMU. She currently works as a producer/director for BBC and has released multiple full-length documentaries. Her most recent film titled "When I Escaped", documents girls from the North Caucasus region in Russia, fleeing their hometown and families in an attempt to escape forced marriage and other oppressive practices.

Living on Water

Re-Visioning the Floating Settlements of Chau Doc, Vietnam

Clara Gardner

As global water levels rise and flooding increases, many floating communities are under threat. One such community is Chau Doc, Vietnam, located in the fertile wetlands of the Mekong Delta. Using Chau Doc as a case study, this essay reviews the intertwined challenges that currently face the community: the impacts of climate change and the increasing demand for water as a resource; the economic competition from larger, more sophisticated aquaculture corporations both in Vietnam and globally, the rise in pollution, and the structural inadequacy of the vernacular housing. Chau Doc is an ideal case study for it both demonstrates the economic and architectural challenges many floating communities currently face and provides a rich foundation from which potential solutions can be investigated.

The creation of floating tourist homestays that attach to Chau Doc's existing home-fisheries is one such solution. This proposal addresses the economic and ecological challenges, specifically those of family-owned, floating aquaculture enterprises. These floating homestays would provide an alternative source of income and seamlessly promote water sanitation by replacing the dumping of untreated household waste with gray and black water treatment systems. These sanitation systems shift the focus of the floating home-fishery typology away from its underwater fish cages and towards protecting the health and wellness of the human inhabitants.

This essay analyzes the existing structures, proposes enhancements for simple, healthy, and sustainable housing, and engages with a climate future where the typology's historic success in living with volatile water flows will be invaluable.

Chau Doc City and the Economics of Catfish Aquaculture

Located in the Mekong Delta's northernmost province, An Giang, Chau Doc is a small, but rapidly growing urban center. Situated at the juncture of the Bassac River, Chau Doc River, and Vinh Te Canal, this urban center is only two kilometers from the Cambodian border. Its position heavily influences the local economy: small fish farms, trade, tourism, and intensive wet-rice farming.

The Mekong Delta has been critical to Vietnam's economic success, producing one-third of Vietnam's GDP, half of its rice, and 70% of its aquaculture (Behr 2019). In the late 1990s, the floating freshwater cage farmers in Chau Doc successfully adapted their traditional, individual family-owned floating fish cages to support intensive catfish aquaculture, producing tons of catfish each year. Studies of global floating cage aquaculture, sponsored by the FAO as early as 2007, correctly predicted that, in Vietnam, the small individual home floating cage model would remain in place "for the foreseeable future" (De Silva and Phillips 2007). By 2005, Vietnam became the world's leading country in the processing and exportation of catfish; and between 2008 and 2016, the number of cages in An Giang increased from 2294 to 5244 (Tuoi Tre News 2021). Today, Chau Doc hosts one of the highest concentrations of floating home-fisheries along the western bank of the Bassac River — an estimated 2000 cages or roughly 600 households, with an average of 3.3 cages per owner/family (Long, Hien, and Phu 2020). According to various sources, a single family can make an average annual operating profit of $23,500 USD p.a. in a decent year. Thus, Chau Doc's floating community can earn an estimated total of $14-15 million USD p.a. in net operating profit, which goes back into Chau Doc's economy (Victoria Hotel Blog 2015).

The success of Chau Doc's intensive catfish aquaculture is linked to the productivity of its floating home-fisheries. With cages floating directly in the River, owners can stock three times the number of fish per cubic meter compared to on-land, artificial ponds. This superior productivity is achieved by using the River's natural flows to constantly flush the densely stacked fish with freshwater for oxygen and for removing feed waste (De Silva and Phillips 2007).

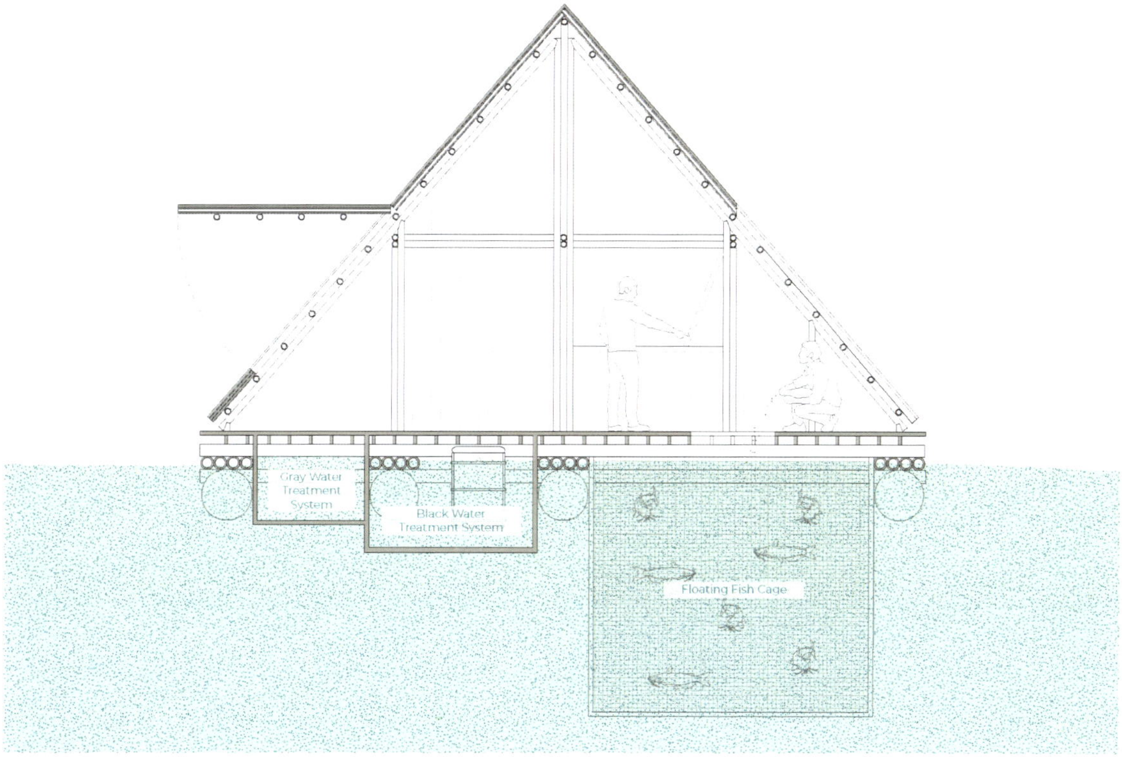

Fig. A
Section of floating A-frame housing incorporating aquaculture

Challenges facing the Floating Home-Fishery Typology

The historic success of Chau Doc's floating fisheries is inextricably linked to the water flow of the Mekong and its distributaries. As such, the effects of climate change and pollution on this fish-dependent community are the most immediate challenges facing Chau Doc, with recent lower water levels posing both direct and indirect risks to the livelihoods of floating communities and their fish.

Flooding and droughts are annual phenomena in the Mekong Delta. Over the past two decades, however, this region has been suffering an overall decline in river water flows, even during the rainy season. In the past, the rainy season accounted for 70-80% of the total annual water flow (Mekong River Commission n.d.). Comparing the Bassac River's highest water level in 2019 to that in 2002, the highest water level was lower by 20% (Mach, Cao, and Cuong n.d.). Furthermore, the flood peak in Chau Doc in 2020 was only 60% of that in 2002. With another low flood season in 2021, the region has not seen a major flood in more than 10 consecutive years. These lower water levels are the result of both climate change (low rainfall) and human manipulation of water flows. While local rainfall contributes to 5% of the water found in the Mekong Delta, 95% of the water comes from upstream sources. Much of this water is currently stored in lakes behind hydroelectric

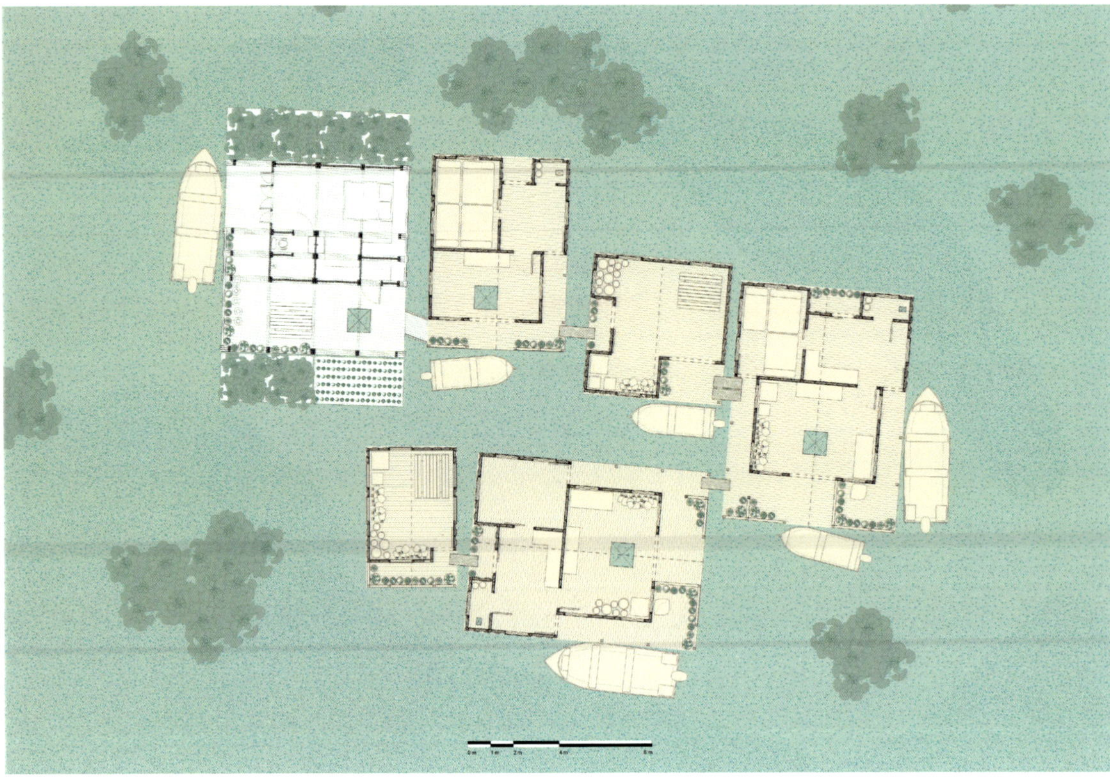

Fig. B
Planimetric view of floating housing cluster

dams (Mach, Cao, and Cuong n.d.). Thus, as demand for irrigation water and energy upstream increases, the water available to the Mekong Delta decreases.

Low water levels directly affect the caged fish in the River, with the extreme drought of 2007 seriously impacting production. In the case of extreme low water levels, oxygen may drop below life sustaining levels and fish suffocate. This occurs when the water flow is reduced to the low oxygen strata found at lower depths and lower velocities. Low water flows over longer periods, even without reaching anoxic levels, increases the chance of disease and slows growth because of exposure to increased concentrations of pollutants (Adamson and Tospornsampan 2008). This in turn reduces family earnings. As a temporary solution, motorboats are positioned next to the cages and run continuously to provide aeration to supply oxygen. This practice continued in the droughts of 2018 and 2019.

Lack of sanitation and water treatment systems are one of the greatest social challenges floating communities in the Mekong Delta face. The most pressing issue is open defecation. Approximately 40% of the families (six million people) in the Mekong Delta use hanging latrines, which drop waste directly into the ponds or rivers below (La 2022). Disposing waste directly into the surface water of

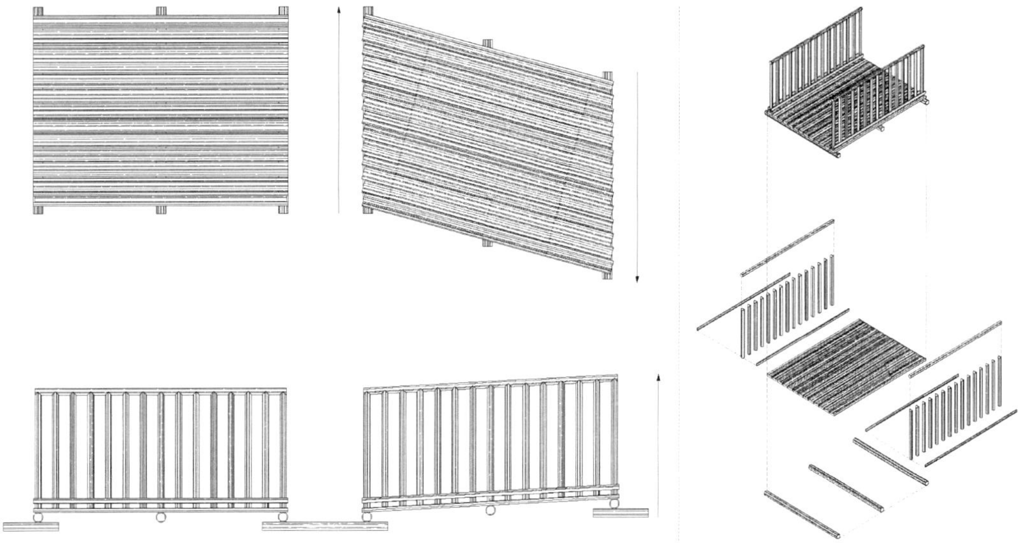

Fig. C
Tectonic Platform
Construction

the Bassac River risks spreading disease to all those who rely on it for water. Yet, invasive water hyacinths (*Eichhornia crassipes*) provide a prolific, natural, and zero-cost absorption filter for the nitrogen and phosphorus pollutants that are created by intensive rice farming, aquaculture, and livestock and human waste disposal into the rivers. Actively supported by UNICEF and NGOs, the Vietnamese government has set nationwide elimination of open defecation by 2025 and 95% access to "safe" sanitation by 2030 as priority goals (Reddy and Sutton 1984).

Homestay Tourism – An Opportunity

Chau Doc City is one of the main economic, political, and cultural centers in An Giang Province. The development of tourism in Chau Doc is prioritized by Vietnam's national and regional governments as a means of supporting urban growth and encouraging rural development to diversify income sources away from traditional rice and aquaculture (Bolay et al. 2019, pg. 620). While tourism has become a major part of the local economy, current tourists are primarily domestic day-trippers who do not spend as much as overnight and international tourists (Bolay et al. 2019, pg. 603 and 628). Promoting international tourism is an attractive option, particularly for Chau Doc with its existing traditional, land-based temples and unique, water-based nature attractions.

The homestay model has become more common in recent years as eco-tourism has become popular. Tourists increasingly want to understand the daily lives and culture of local inhabitants. Given the prioritization of international tourism by Chau Doc's regional government, simultaneously expanding the tourist experience and the floating home's income by incorporating eco-homestay style tourist accommodations into the floating community offers a practical and attractive option.

Fig. D
Gray Water
Treatment System

The Proposal – A Floating Homestay

Floating homestays can provide alternate income for the local families by balancing declining aquaculture income caused by longer, more intense droughts and high-tech, land-based competition. These homestays also aim to adapt and preserve the floating housing typology through the addition of gray and black water treatment systems. These floating units would be owned by individual families who would work in conjunction with local tour operators.

This intervention focuses on the design of a single floating homestay unit, characterized by a private enclosed bedroom, bathroom, and an exterior covered veranda for eating and relaxing. The inclusion of a fish cage under the veranda would allow tourists to more accurately experience the owners' day-to-day life. However, unlike the existing home-fisheries, whose floating fish cage is accessible via a floor hatch in the main room, the fish cage under the homestay unit would be accessed outside the guests' primary living areas, separating public and private space.

Fig. E
Black Water
Treatment System

This A-framed structure (8.5 meters long by 8.6 meters wide, and 5 meters above water), is designed to merge with the owners' home next door. Its steep pitched roof directs rainwater runoff, which is necessary during the monsoon season. The A-frame structure also lowers the floating platform's center of gravity, making it more stable in turbulent water. Occupant safety is addressed by replacing simple wooden planks that stretch between floating platforms with railed, tectonic walkways. These tectonic connections allow the floating platforms to be more flexible.
The existing home-fishery and proposed homestay unit are both constructed using the post and lintel system. Rather than wood framing, however, the floating homestay uses bamboo columns and beams that are bundled together for structural stability. By bundling these elements together, the bamboo is able to span longer distances. Walls are constructed out of halved culms of bamboo that are then fastened together using horizontal strips.

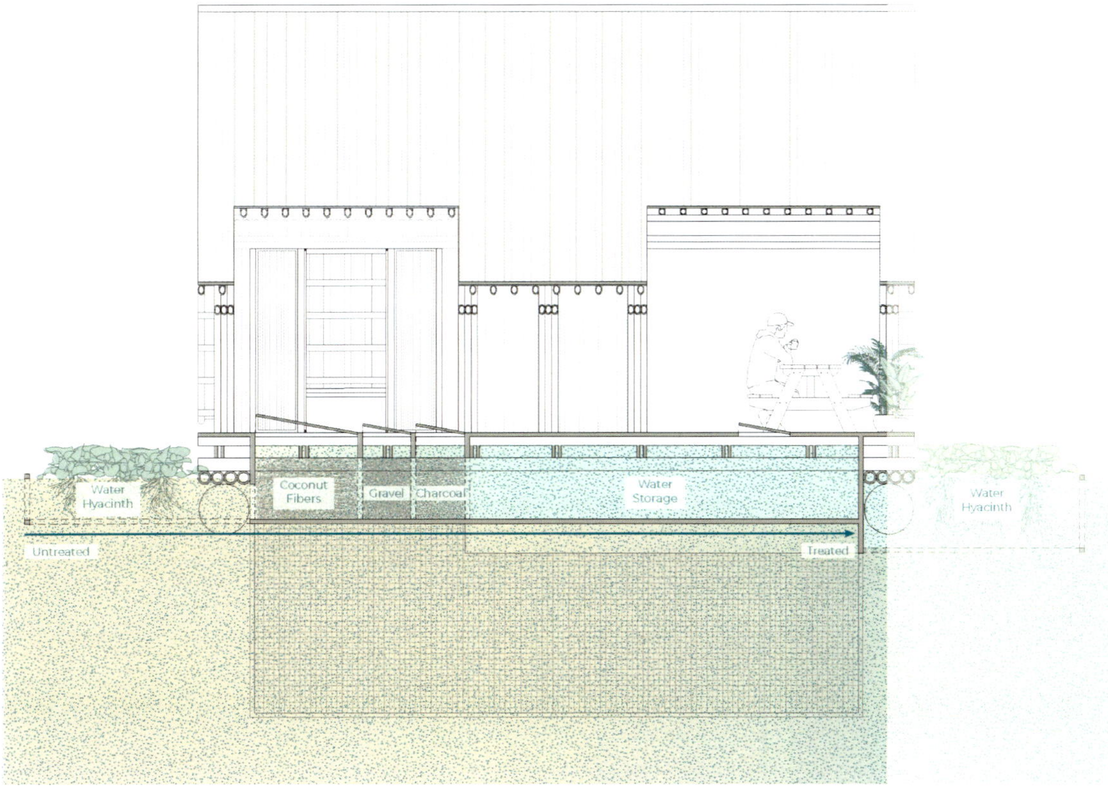
Water Hyacinth
Coconut Fibers
Gravel
Charcoal
Water Storage
Water Hyacinth
Untreated
Treated

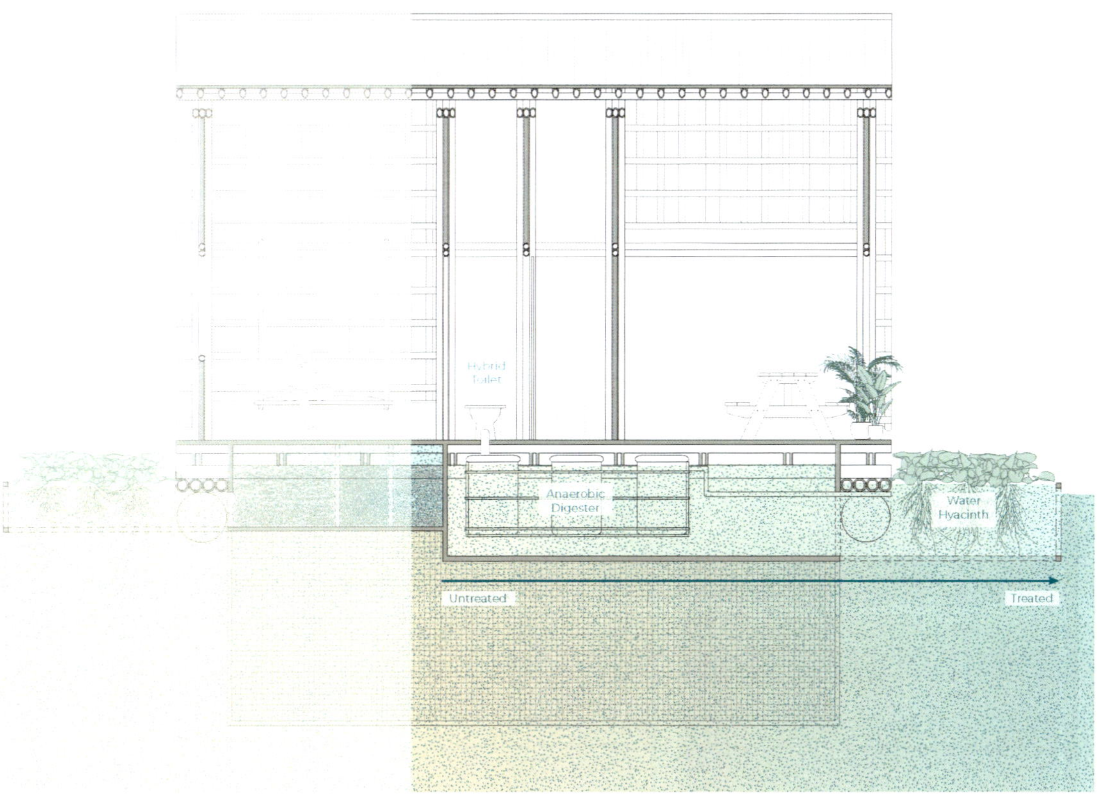
Hybrid Toilet
Anaerobic Digester
Water Hyacinth
Untreated
Treated

Homestays are most successful when they draw structurally and aesthetically from tradition and blend with the current typology. The use of vernacular, locally sourced materials impacts more than just the superficial. While ironwood is one of the primary woods used in the construction of floating fish cages, it is overexploited, expensive, and illegal to use. Thus, it is necessary to transition to ethical, affordable, locally sourced materials, such as spiny bamboo. This switch to bamboo modifies the construction technique of the floating system, shifting from a log-float system to a pontoon system that uses a combination of structural bamboo and plastic water drums for flotation.

Finally, sanitation and water treatment systems are the most critical upgrades in this floating homestay unit. There are two proposed water treatment systems: gray water and black water. The gray water system uses the natural flow of the river to push the water through a filtration system of water hyacinths, coconut fibers, gravel, and charcoal. Black water is treated separately in a series of anaerobic digesters and is then emptied into a pond of water hyacinths. This black water treatment system is derived from the HandyPod, developed for floating homes in Cambodia (Wetlands Work n.d.). These additions actively shift the focus of the typology away from its commercial aquaculture to protecting the health and wellness of its human inhabitants.

Conclusion

As an incremental intervention that focuses on stabilizing the livelihoods and boosting the physical wellbeing of Chau Doc's historic floating fishing community, these homestay units may be one approach to preserving this housing typology in vulnerable water-based communities. Nevertheless, it is important to acknowledge the potential drawbacks of this proposal, particularly as it pertains to tourism and the environment. Economically, tourism has many benefits, especially for rapidly growing urban areas. However, while supported by the Vietnamese government for these reasons, tourism also has the potential to negatively affect the immediate environment and local community.

Ha Long Bay in the north of Vietnam offers a cautionary tale of the effects of tourism in a World Heritage environment. Much more heavily trafficked than Chau Doc, with approximately 500 daily and overnight tourist boat tours, Ha Long Bay suffers from environmental waste management issues. Most of the Bay's pollution originates from tour boats' diesel fuel, tourist trash, and discharge from the growing urban city of Ha Long. Yet government efforts to maintain this site in the wake of tourism have been draconian — the 2013 removal and relocation of the local population from the Bay's four historic floating villages in the name of a "cleaner environment." Individuals were later permitted to return during the day to their refurbished floating houses to participate in controlled tourist "presentations" (Halong Hub 2020).

As the tale of Ha Long Bay's pollution illustrates, the temporary influx of non-native visitors results in both positive consequences, boosting the local economy, but also serious negative impacts, the stress placed on natural resources and the environment and the displacement of local communities. Thus, this proposal for Chau Doc's floating homestays seeks to thoughtfully mitigate the negative issues by integrating eco-tourism within the daily lives of the local community, incorporating water treatment systems, and promoting the use of locally sourced, sustainable materials. Thus, these simple, everyday housing structures above the fish cages have the potential to become prototypes for a more sustainable future.

References:

Adamson, P.A. and J. Tospornsampan. "Annual Mekong Flood Report 2007." Mekong River Commission (MRC). Vientiane, Lao PDR: MRC, 2008.

"An Insider's Look into a Floating Fish Farm in the Mekong Delta." *Victoria Hotel* (blog). June 1, 2015. https://www.victoriahotels.asia/en/news/an-insiders-look-into-a-floating-fish-farm-in-the-mekong-delta/.

Behr, Diji Chandrasekharan. "Vietnam and the Mekong Delta: Drafting a Plan to Ensure Greater Productivity and Climate-Resilience." *World Bank Blogs* (blog). October 1, 2019. https://blogs.worldbank.org/en/eastasiapacific/vietnam-and-mekong-delta-drafting-plan-ensure-greater-productivity-and-climate.

Bolay, Jean-Claude, Labattut Eléonore, Ngo Than Loan, and Nguyen Hoang My Lan. "Local Sustainable Development Indicators and Urbanization in Vietnam, What Are the Good Questions? The Case of the City of Chau Doc in the Mekong Delta." *Current Urban Studies* 7, no. 4 (2019): 598 – 636. https://doi.org/10.4236/cus.2019.74032.

De Silva, Sena and Michael Phillips. "A Review of Cage Aquaculture: Asia (Excluding China)." *Cage Aquaculture - Regional Reviews and Global Overview* 498 (2007): 18 – 48.

"Floating Village Sanitation." Wetlands Work website. https://www.wetlandswork.com/floating-village-sanitation.

La, Minh-Ha, "Ten facts about sanitation in Vietnam." *The Borgen Report* (blog). February 4, 2022. https://borgenproject.org/10-facts-about-sanitation-in-vietnam/.

Long, Nguyen Thanh, Huynh Van Hien, and Tran Minh Phu. "The Status of Basa Fish *Pangasius Bocourti* in Cage Culture in An Giang Province, Vietnam." *International Journal of Scientific and Research Publications* (IJSRP) 10, no. 10 (2020): 71 – 77.

Mach, Le Thu, Hoang Long Cao, and Vu The Cuong. "Floods and Migrants of Vietnam's Mekong Delta." *Earth Journalism Network*. February 9, 2022. https://earthjournalism.net/stories/floods-and-migrants-of-vietnams-mekong-delta-25-lessons-from-the-data.

"Mekong Delta: A 35-Year Miracle Change of Vietnam's Rice Bowl." Tuoi Tre News. February 6, 2021. https://tuoitrenews.vn/news/features/20210206/mekong-delta-a-35year-miracle-change-of-vietnams-rice-bowl/59135.html.

"Mekong River Commission For Sustainable Development." MRC website. https://www.mrcmekong.org.

Reddy, K.R. and D.L. Sutton. "Water Hyacinths for Water Quality Improvement and Biomass Production." *Journal of Environmental Quality* 13, no. 1 (1984): 1 – 8. https://doi.org/10.2134/jeq1984.00472425001300010001x.

"What's the Story behind Halong Bay's Floating Villages?" Halong Hub (blog), June 2, 2020. https://www.halonghub.com/blog/halong-bay-amazing-floating-villages/.

About the Author

Clara Gardner graduated with a Bachelor of Architecture from Tulane University in 2023. Her honor's thesis, "Living on Water: Re-Visioning the Floating Settlements of Chau Doc, Vietnam, through the Implementation of Homestay Tourism," examines the current ecological and economic challenges facing floating fishery communities in the Mekong Delta, Vietnam, from climate change and from increasingly sophisticated competition in aquaculture. Born in Vietnam, adopted by a single-mother, and raised in New York City, this thesis was inspired both by Gardner's architectural interest in traditional floating housing and her desire to learn more about her birth country, its culture, and the challenges that currently face some of its more vulnerable communities.

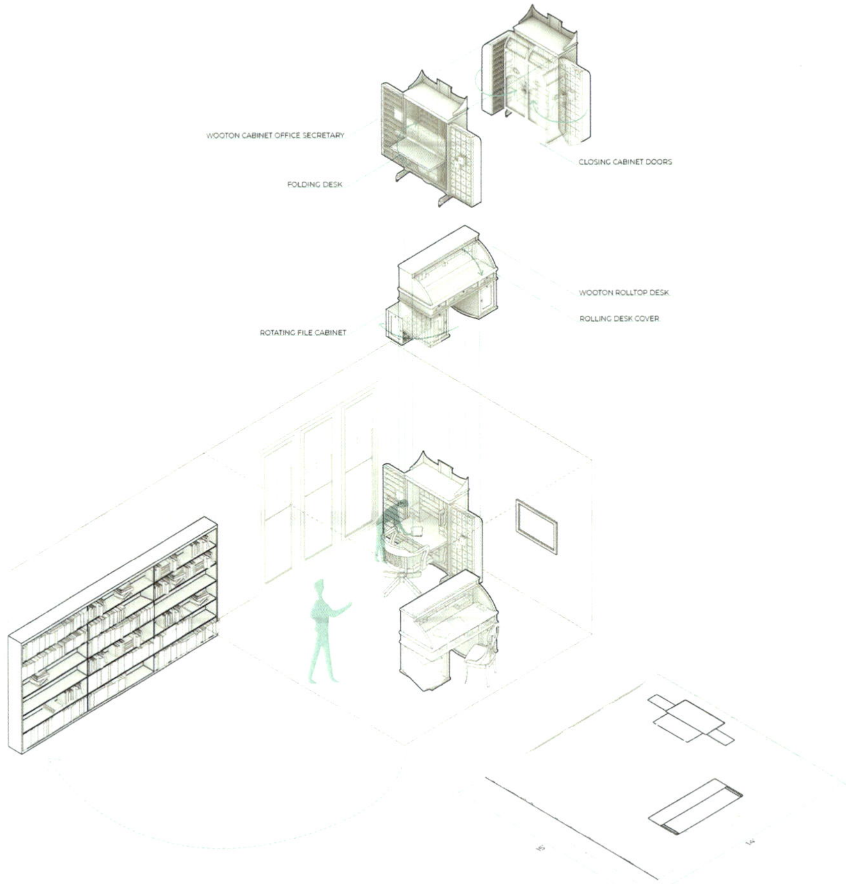
WOOTON CABINET OFFICE SECRETARY
FOLDING DESK
CLOSING CABINET DOORS
WOOTON ROLLTOP DESK
ROLLING DESK COVER
ROTATING FILE CABINET

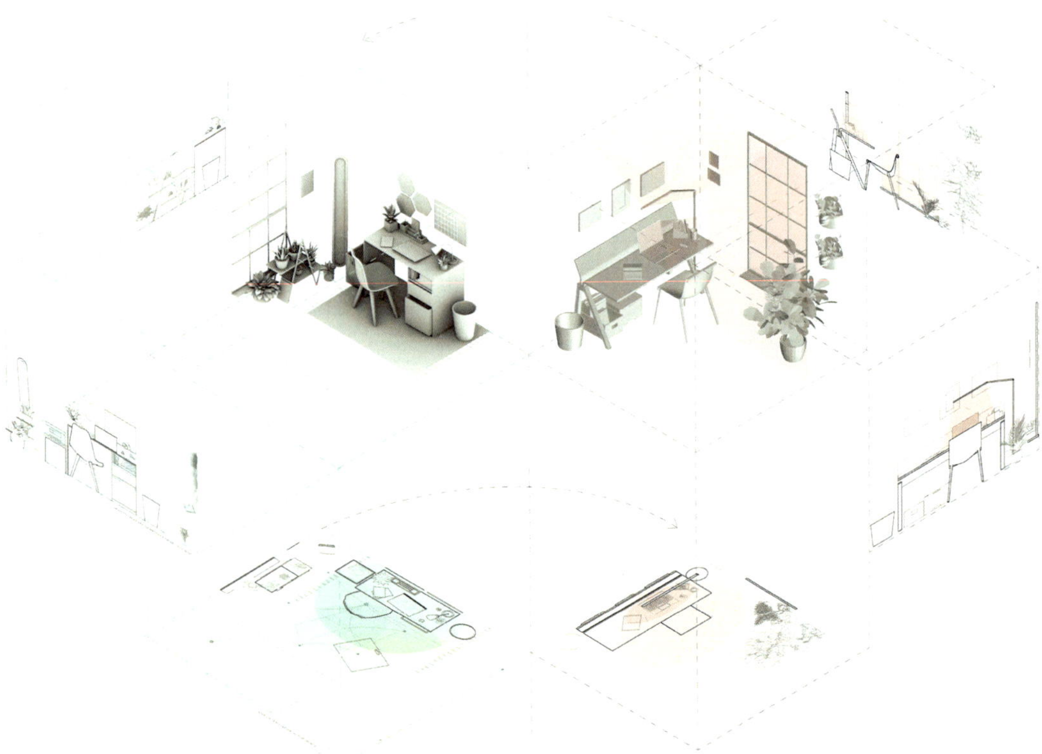

Fig. A
Merchant's Office "Unit of Work" — Drawing by Jesse Auer

OOO to RTO: Lessons Learned from Workspace Evolutions

Katie Stranix

Fig. B
Home Office "Unit of Work" - Drawing by Leah Kirssin and Jesse Auer

What will become of the office? Once an integral part of the everyday lives of most Americans, this omnipresent typology has become increasingly vacant and underutilized in the wake of the COVID-19 pandemic. These core and shell structures define the skylines of major cities and dominate the rentable floor area of most downtowns. Many companies are requiring at least a partial return to their physical domains, forcing these structures to readjust yet again to new spatial demands and social expectations. Despite this trend, occupancy levels will most likely fail to return to their pre-COVID peak as employees petition for locational flexibility and as AI continues to replace human workers in more sectors. What are the spatial implications of society's shifting attitude towards the workplace? What can we learn from prior evolutions of this typology and the influence of previous shifts on the spatial lineage of the office?

Workplace environments evolve over time not only in response to improved building methods, material innovations, and technological advancements, but also to broader cultural, economic, and legislative influences. These developments not only heavily impact the physical extents of the collective workplace, but the architectural elements that shape the territory of the individual are also largely determined by the employer-employee dynamic and the dominant societal values of the time.

In the late 19th century, master and apprentice coexisted in the same space, often a singular room. With the introduction of Scientific Management in the early 20th century, the factory-like division of labor increased the number of employees, introducing middle management into the relationship. This influx in workers triggered the initial embrace of the open plan, optimal for its efficiency and increased visibility and surveillance. The introduction of private, cellular offices, often positioned along the building's façade, spatially expressed corporate hierarchies, offering both views into the central pool of clerks and stenos and out to the surrounding urban or rural landscape.

Fig. C
Cubicle Office "Unit of Work" — Drawing by Trenton Rhodes

Following World War II, many companies in Europe turned away from hierarchical spatial concepts and embraced the democratic ideals of the Burolandschaft movement. Flow of information and departmental adjacencies guided the seemingly haphazard arrangement of desks creating organic clusters of workers rather than uniform columns. The term "knowledge worker" was coined by Peter Drucker, describing autonomous employees capable of self-management. Employee and employer inhabited the same plane, both intellectually and physically, becoming team members, working together towards shared goals. In line with this trend in the early 1960s, Robert Probst developed the Action Office system, giving more personal control to the worker and more versatility to the open workspace. This valiant attempt at flexibility and autonomy was eventually undermined by its cheaper and more rigid cousin, the cubicle, a modular system of pseudo-rooms that dominated office interiors of the late 1980s and early 90s. Its introduction brought about the return of the perimeter office, injecting hierarchy to the workspace once again. And although workers had the ability to personalize their spaces with mementos, they had little control over the physical bounds of their workspace. The monotony and placelessness of the cubicle farm paired with deep floorplates, endless acoustic ceiling tile, and lack of access to natural light and views, prompted a return to the open office plan and a desire for healthier and more novel office environments.

Fig. D
Second Home LA by Selgascano "Unit of Work" — Drawing by Meghann McMahon

The concept of office as campus emerged in the early 2000s with the rise of the tech industry and proliferation of laptop computers, untethering workers from the territory of their desks. Collective spaces for recreation and relaxation began to populate the floor plan, introducing non-work-related programs and spaces to the office. The development of these amenity spaces was spurred by competition for top talent within the workforce, encouraging employers to create unique, exciting, and inviting spaces focused

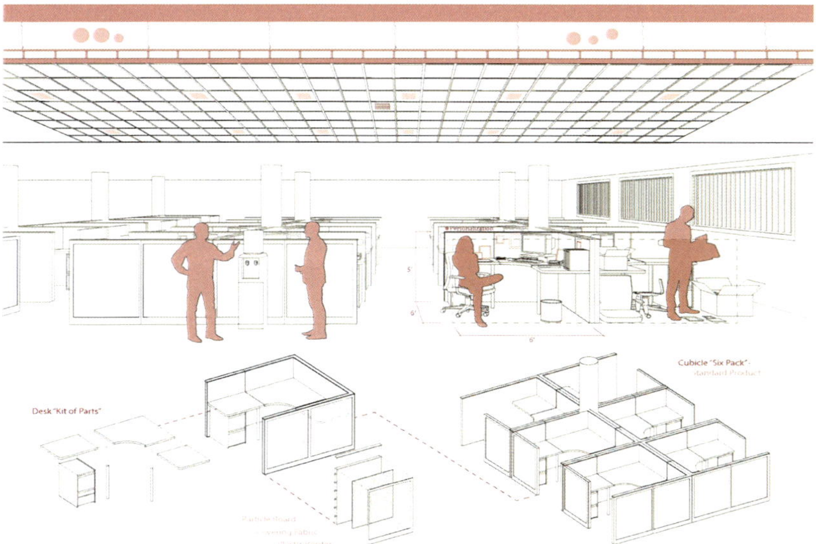

UNITS OF WORK

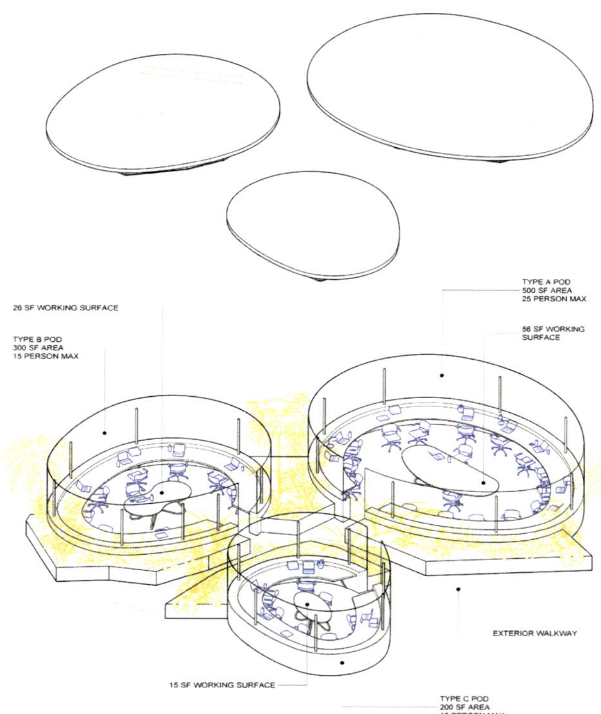

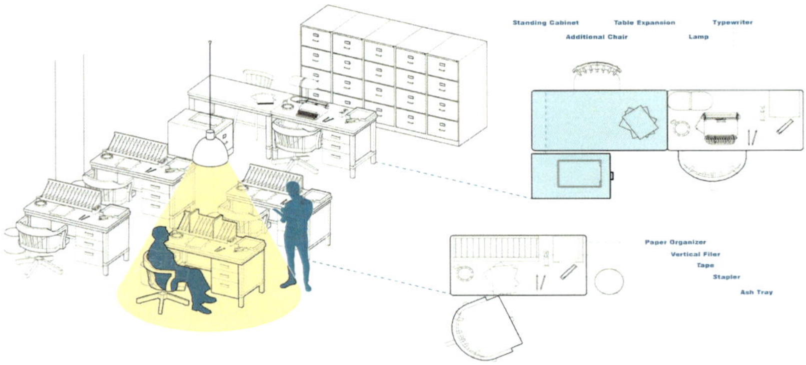

Fig. E
Taylorist Office "Unit of Work" - Drawing by Trenton Rhodes

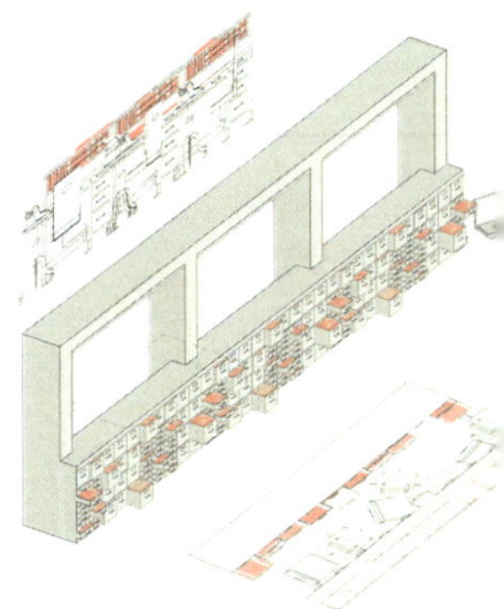

Fig. F
Larkin Building "Unit of Work" - Drawing by Leah Kirssin

not only on employee productivity, but also their satisfaction and enjoyment. Coworking spaces, arriving with the increase in remote work in the late aughts and 2010s, took this concept one step further by rebranding themselves as social clubs, requiring spaces not only for work, but also for communal activities and events.

In early 2020, the pandemic forced an abrupt shift to remote working for many knowledge workers in America and throughout the world. It required people to carve out a space for work within their domestic environments, giving them more control over certain aspects of their space while merging the two typically separate realms. Working within this space for the duration of the pandemic and beyond has altered the dynamic between employer and employee yet again. Workers now have more agency over where and when they work and less tolerance for endless hours in the office. The comforts of domestic space are crossing over into office interiors to ease the transition between home and work and to offer the same kind of atmosphere without the distractions of everyday life. The fusion of once separate domains has the potential to erode typological traits and create new synergies between seemingly disparate programs. Will the office building continue to evolve as a distinct type or will it dissolve as work becomes more flexible, fluid, and integrated into everyday life?

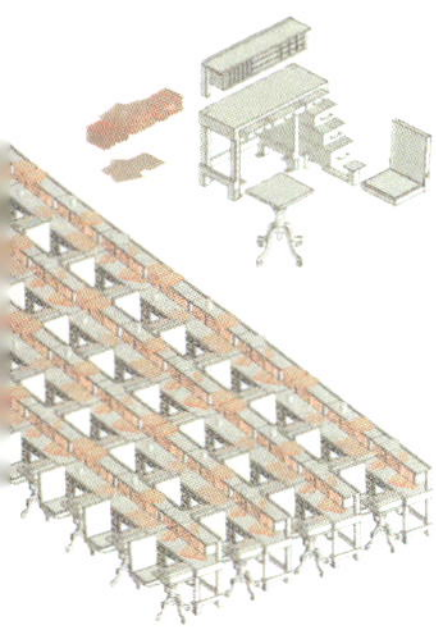

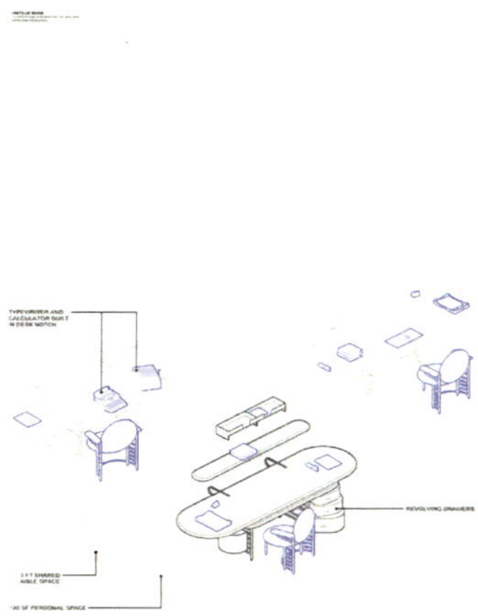

Fig. G
Johnson Wax "Unit of Work" - Drawing by Meghann McMahon

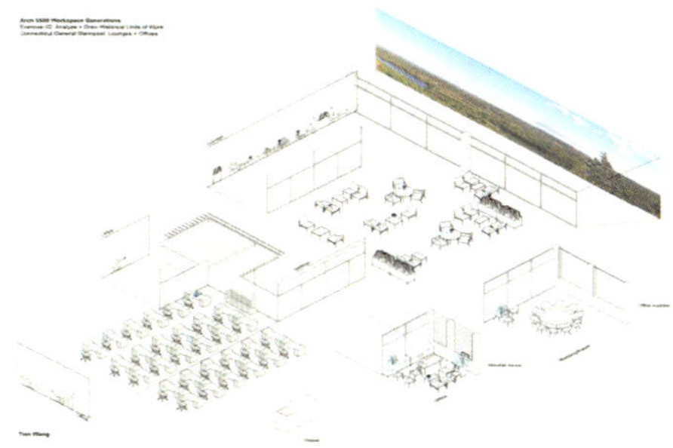

Fig. H
Stenopool "Unit of Work" - Drawing by Leah Kirssin

The hybridization of the office typology with others is not new, particularly given its interior flexibility. The Schiller Building by Louis Sullivan and Dankmar Adler built in Chicago in 1891 and unfortunately demolished in 1961, housed a full theater beneath its office spaces. Office floors stacked on top of the 1300 seat theater and fly tower, making the lobby the primary shared space and social catalyst for theater-goers and office occupants. Price Tower by Frank Lloyd Wright built in 1956 in Bartlesville, Oklahoma experimented with ideas around live-work by embedding double-height residences amidst single-story private offices. A later renovation converted the apartments into exhibition spaces and offices into hotel rooms, shifting away from live-work, but continuing unconventional pairings. Kevin Roche and John Dinkeloo merged greenhouse and office at the Ford Foundation in the late 1960s in New York City. Visitors and employees pass through the green space prior to entering the domain of the office, a welcome break from the urban surroundings. A conventional building corridor is reconceived as a dynamic pedestrian street in Stockholm's SAS Headquarters by Niels Torp, built in 1987. This connective space engages the surrounding structures, making the headquarters feel like a small town rather than sprawling building. Selgascano architects disperses the office within a garden at the Second Home office in LA, completed in 2020.

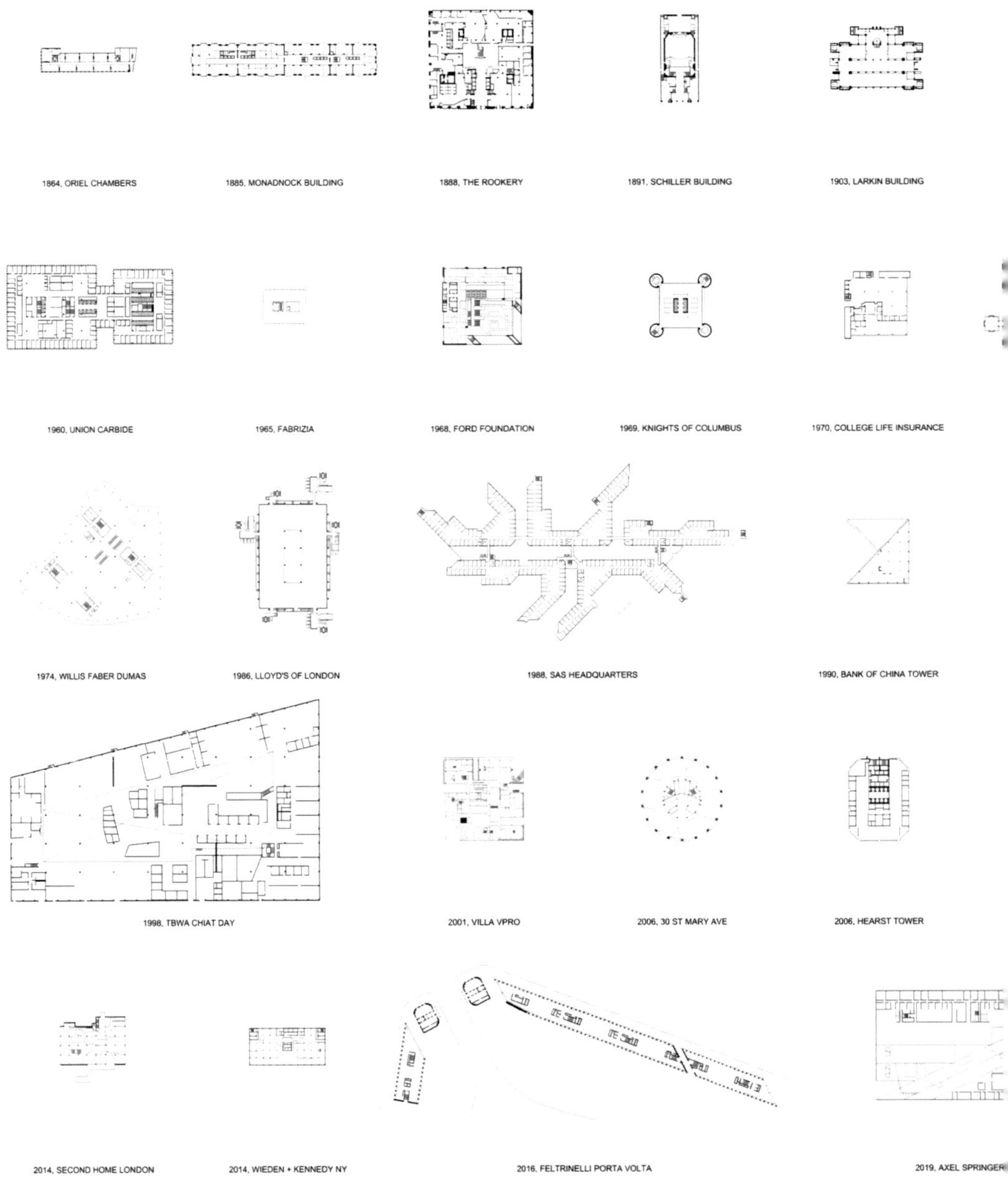

Fig. I
Office Plans - Drawn by Audrey Liu and Meghann McMahon

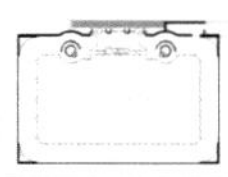

1939, JOHNSON WAX

1952, LEVER HOUSE

1956, PRICE TOWER

1957, INLAND STEEL BUILDING

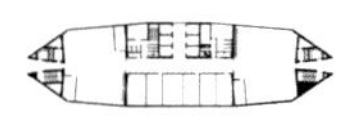

1958, PIRELLI ADMIN BUILDING

1974, SEARS TOWER

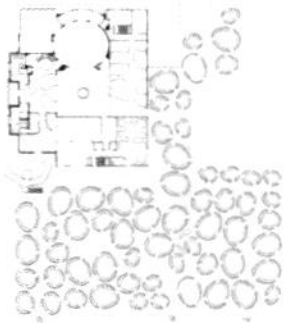

2019, SECOND HOME LA

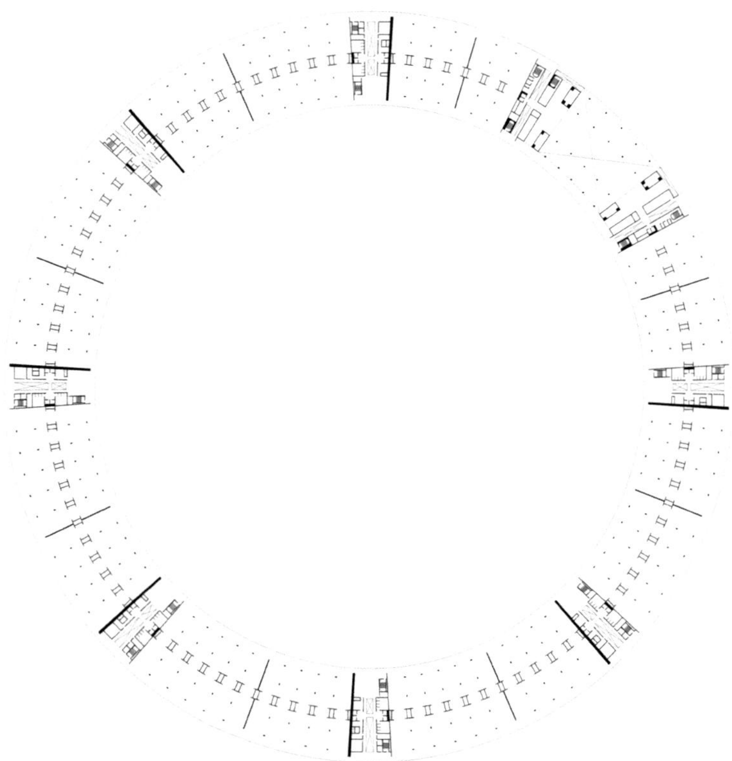

2017, APPLE PARK

Coworkers occupy pods encircled by garden paths and immersed in vegetation confusing the boundary between interior and exterior space. These juxtapositions and productive adjacencies impact the spatial organization of each project as well as the overall form, creating enhanced everyday environments that engage a diversity of users.

Fig. J
Action Office 1
"Unit of Work" –
Drawing by Jolie Magenheimer

The cyclical pattern of open to cellular, cellular to open, has been permanently derailed by COVID-19, launching us into a new paradigm altogether. The changing social, economic, political, and environmental climate demands a response from the built environment, particularly from the structures that dominate our cities and suburbs. Past evolutions can offer insight into potential futures, inspiring dynamic and novel territories where the employee-employer relationship can continue to evolve.

About the Author

Katie Stranix is an Assistant Professor of Architecture at the University of Virginia and a registered architect, principal, and co-founder of Office of Things, PLLC, a collaborative architecture office based in New York, Chicago, and Charlottesville. Prior to joining UVA and founding Office of Things, she worked as a project architect and design team member at Studio Gang Architects — first in New York and later in their Chicago office — on a range of projects including the Solar Carve Tower and the Richard Gilder Center for Science, Education, and Innovation at the American Museum of Natural History. Her work as both an educator and practitioner of architecture focuses on the transformation and enrichment of everyday spaces within our shared built environment, identifying opportunities for the insertion of playful and inviting spaces, structures, and sequences that enhance our individual and collective physical and mental health.

Fig. K
Vitra Workstation Components
"Unit of Work" –
Drawing by Jolie Magenheimer

The drawings included here were produced by UVA students, JT Bachman, and Katie Stranix as part of the Workspace Futures project, a multi-year research effort in partnership with Google investigating the spatial implications of the changing nature of work. The research began in 2019 with two seminars, Workspace Evolutions and Workspace Generations, and culminated in an exhibit at the UVA School of Architecture in the fall of 2022.

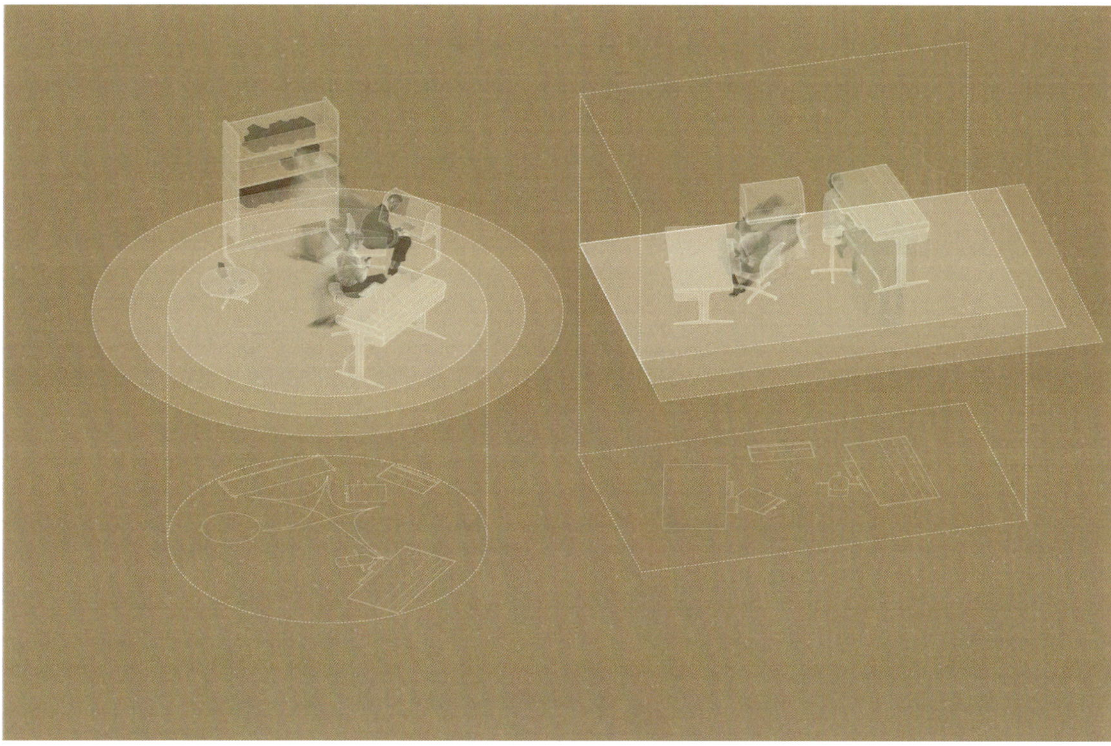

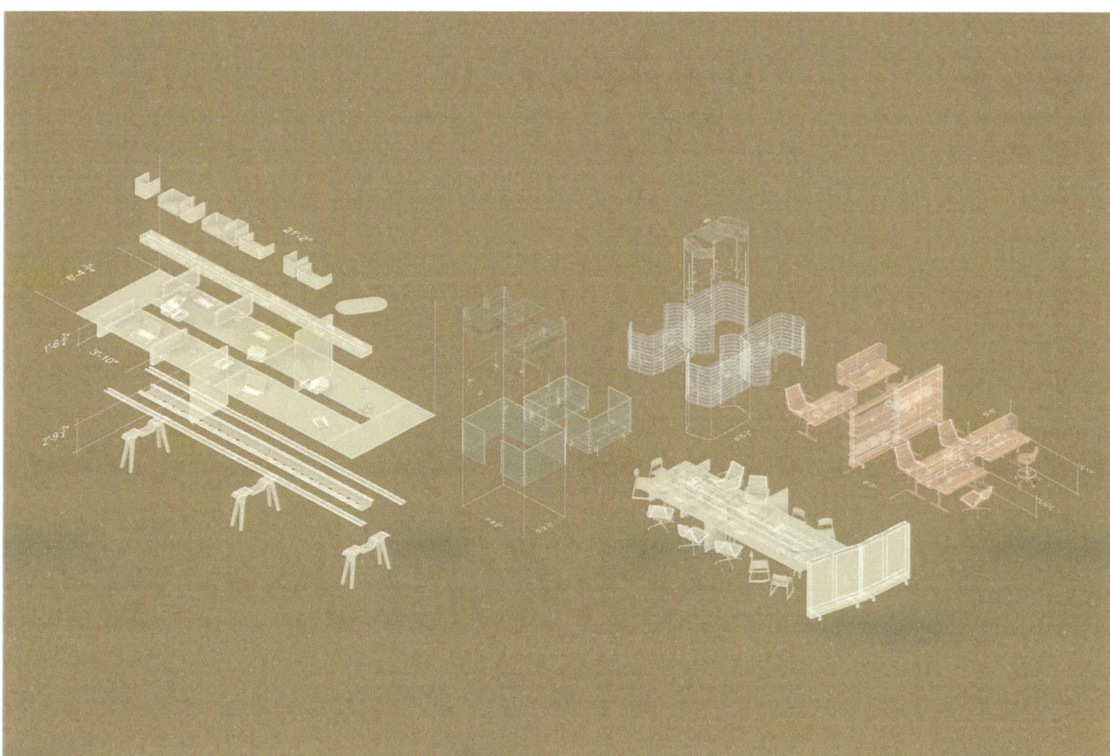

A Monthly Review of the Ice,
Ice Making Refrigerating Cold Storage
and Kindred Trades

Vol. XXVII. No. 3. CHICAGO : NEW YORK, SEPTEMBER 1, 1

No. 3. CHICAGO : NEW YORK, SEPTEMBER 1, 1904. $2.00

[Written and Illustrated Expressly for ICE AND REFRIGERATION.]

Refrigerating Plants at Louisiana Purch

MODEL DAIRY AND REFRIGERATION IN CONNECTION—COLD STORAGE APPLES—REFRIGERATI
—IN FISH AND FISHERIES—COOLING MISSOURI STATE BUILDING—REFRIGERATION IN
TAURANT, IN INSIDE INN, ETC.—EXHIBIT OF REFRIGERATING AND ICE MAKING MA

THE World's Fair at St. Louis is two-thirds over and ICE AND REFRIGERATION is informed that some of the participants or concessionaires have figured out that [illegible]

is so uneven or hilly that to ation needed from a centr costly installation of machi [illegible]

Thermal Comfort

Shirley (Dongwei) Chen

Mechanically conditioned air was an everyday invention. As Reyner Banham observed in *The Architecture of the Well-Tempered Environment*, it took almost four decades from the first industrial uses of air-conditioning, for famous architects such as Frank Lloyd Wright to confidently employ the technology (Banham 1969, pg. 27). Sixty-five years before Banham's published *The Architecture of the Well-Tempered Environment*, a trade magazine dedicated its third issue to the refrigerating plant at the 1904 Louisiana Purchase Exposition in St. Louis, Missouri. "A monthly review of the ice, ice making, refrigerating, and kindred trades," *Ice and Refrigeration* covered issues from ice cream storage temperature to ice house roofing techniques (Ice and Refrigeration 1904, pg. 81).

The American public experienced centralized cooling for the first time in history at the 1904 exposition (DOE 2015). This new era of indoor comfort was marked by the installation of a 30-ton refrigeration plant in the basement of the Missouri State Building. To keep the exhibition hall four to six degrees cooler than outdoors, 35,000 cubic feet of mechanically chilled air was pumped through galvanized iron conduits per minute. The cooling process required four thousand feet of cooling pipes, twelve drums of anhydrous ammonia, and a seven-foot motorized blast wheel. Above this maze of mechanized environmental control systems, the fairgoers enjoyed a splendid view of a ten-foot-tall fountain in the building's rotunda, a visual reminder of their newly gained access to indoor climate control (Ice and Refrigeration 1904, pg. 96-97).

Since the 1904 World's Fair, conditioned air has breezed through interiors across the United States, from private homes to office towers. "The history of environmental management by the consumption of power in regenerative installations, rather than by simple reliance on conservative and selective structures, is thus a predominantly American history" (Banham 1969, pg. 26). At $99, one could purchase a self-installing window-mounted AC unit on Amazon today. Unlike the early-twentieth-century fairgoers, we are no longer in awe of the magic power of mechanically conditioned air. Instead, its hum fades away as the background track for our daily chores. We are reminded of its presence, when a random drip of water lands on our cheek from the neighbor's AC unit above the sidewalk, much like the drizzle from the ten-foot-tall fountain in the Missouri State Building a century ago. The environmental cost of mechanized indoor climate control, whether in 2023 or 1904, remains an afterthought.

Fig. A
Cover of Ice and Refrigeration XXVII, Issue no. 3 (September 1904).

Fig. B
Screenshot of sound pattern generated from an indoor AC unit.

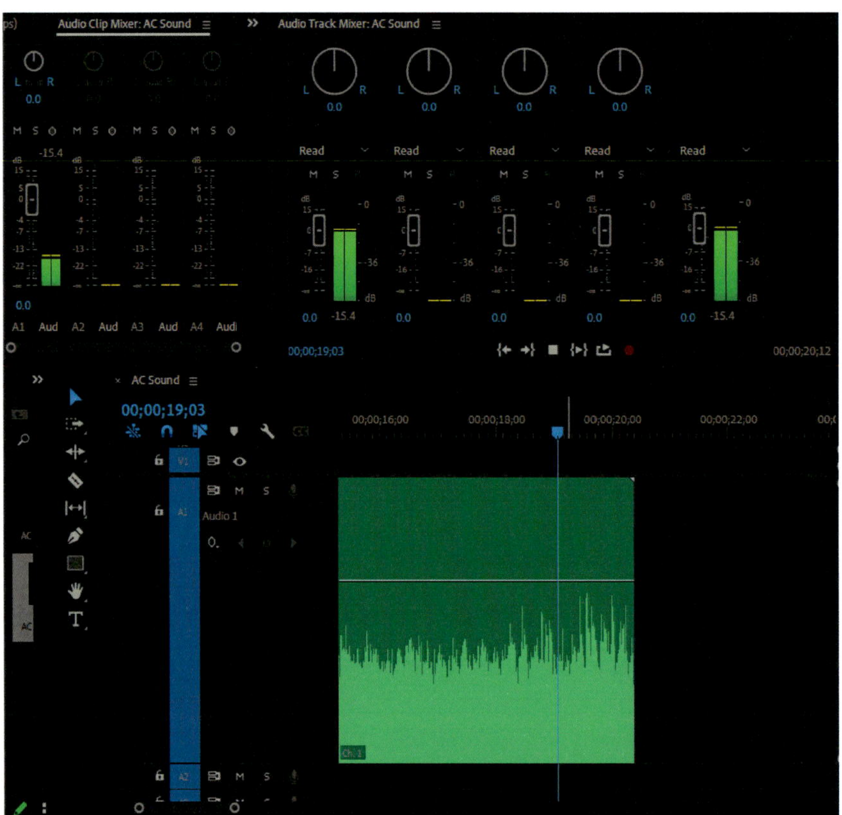

Vol.27 ∴ No.3
THE NEW YORK PUBLIC LIBRARY
September, 1904
Ice and Refrigeration
Illustrated
Science Unites the Antipodes
N
W
E
S
Nickerson & Collins Co.
Publishers
Chicago and New York

References:

Banham, Reyner. *The Architecture of the Well-Tempered Environment*. London: Architectural Press, 1969.

"History of Air Conditioning." Department of Energy (DOE). July 20, 2015. https://www.energy.gov/articles/history-air-conditioning.

"Refrigerating Plants at Louisiana Purchase Exposition." *Ice and Refrigeration* 27, no. 3, September 1904.

About the Author

Shirley (Dongwei) Chen is an architectural designer based in New York and a recent graduate from Princeton School of Architecture, where she is an editor of Pidgin and co-host of psoa radio. Her works have been exhibited at a83, New York, Tbilisi Architecture Biennale, and Trinity Buoy Wharf, London, and her writings have been included in Utzonia: From / To Denmark with Love, Yale Paprika!, and Princeton Tortoise. Shirley is one half of design collaborative DoZa.

Co-designing Everyday Things

Human Parameters in Circular Design: Chair No. 7

Ehsan Baharlou

In architectural design, the model of design to construction is constantly changing. One parameter in these permanent changes is human need, such as a sustainable environment. To address climate change, conventional building methods that follow the linear economy, "take-make-dispose," are being challenged by other methods such as circular construction. Circular construction adopts the 3R approach, "reduce-reuse-recycle," effectively and innovatively using local resources to reuse waste materials. Circularity in the production of goods challenges both mass production and mass customization, providing an opportunity to center human needs in the production of everyday things.

Computational design allows the integration of material and fabrication techniques into the design process. It can serve as an interface to incorporate human parameters as an integral part of circular construction. This interface embraces design agency while the generated design is within the constructible space. This essay presents the development of a computational interface specifically developed to work within the circular construction process. Through a case study, it illustrates the production process of everyday things, such as a chair.

Fig. A
The chair in use

Introduction to the Circular use of Plastic

The short history of using plastic in architecture goes back to the Monsanto house of the future (1957) (Faircloth 2015). This project presents structural capabilities of composite plastic in the construction of curved shapes. It was an attempt to introduce plastic as a structural element to the building industry. Today plastic materials in various forms—including thermoplastics, thermosets, and elastomers—are commonly used in building construction. They are used indirectly as construction molds or directly as building facades or interior spaces. Recent use of plastic composites such as carbon fiber-reinforced polymers (CFRP) presents the undeniable potential of their use in building structural elements (Menges and Knippers 2021). This material's irreplaceability makes it impossible to envision a world without plastic (Meikle 1995). The long biodegradation of plastic necessitates changing the mindset about plastics use.

In 2018, the EPA announced that plastic waste is 12.2% of the municipal solid waste, of which only 4.47% is recycled (EPA 2023a) . Reducing the Toxics Release Inventory (TRI) of plastic production is a promising indication of fruition efforts (EPA 2023b). For example, we can discuss the efforts at the scale of the University of Virginia (UVA)'s community. UVA's 2020-2030 Sustainability Plan aims to reduce the waste footprints of UVA's community by 30%

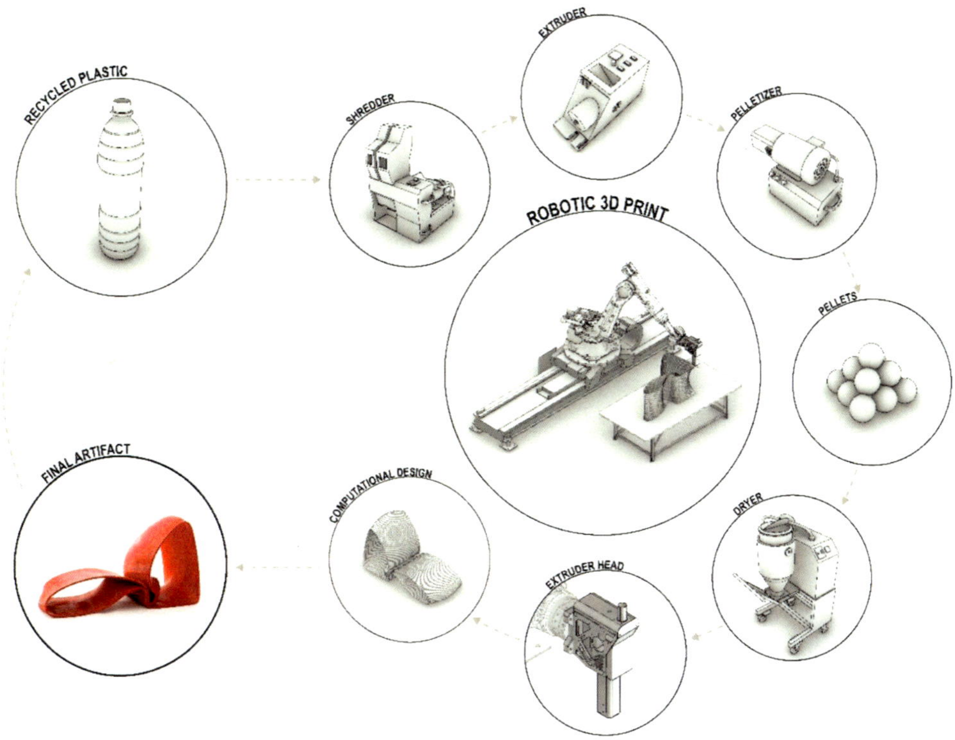

Fig. B
A schematic diagram proposing the implementation of circular construction on a robotically 3D printed chair.

of 2010 levels, which includes plastic waste (University of Virginia 2022). UVA's Recycling Division collects plastic waste on a daily basis. Plastics are classified into groups numbered 1 through 7 based on their recyclability. In the recycling division, the sorting of plastic waste by category is outsourced for further recycling.

Novel approaches like Cradle to Cradle (McDonough and Braungart 2002) and Circular Economy (Ellen MacArthur Foundation 2013) propose the design and implementation of a sustainable approach in manufacturing. Circularity in production invests in the efficient use of resources through innovation in repurposing waste materials. This approach challenges the linear model of economy, "take-make-waste" (Leonard and Conrad 2010), by introducing the circular model of economy. The circular economy includes reducing, reusing, and recycling (3R) to decrease raw materials and residual waste (Cheshire 2021). Extending the circular economy into construction highlights the importance of design-to-fabrication agencies. In the reusing stage, this is the designer who, with available tools, revitalizes the ready-to-dispose artifacts. Reusing thermoplastic wastes can be simplified into shredding and binding reground plastics and can include methods such as extruding them with virgin plastic. This simple type of recycling process enables the examination of the circular construction on a small scale.

Examining circular construction with recycled plastic on a small scale allows individualization in making. This process focuses on identifying parameters that can be individualized to provide human needs in interaction with the surrounding environment. The question is which parameters should be chosen based on what criteria. Can providing easy access to hardware and software to integrate these parameters be effective in making everyday objects?

From Shredding to Extruding Thermoplastic

Fig. C
Rotated side view of the 3D printed chair, illustrating the seating length and the adjustment of the back to the body's curvature.

Technological advancements in the additive manufacturing industry, including 3D printing, facilitate easier access to this technology for everybody. For instance, 3D printing parts can be purchased at reasonable prices and easily assembled by following open-access instructions. Such accessibility to building 3D printers allows enthusiasts to design and actively participate in the process of formation and materialization. This democratization process provides universal access to 3D printing technologies. Such accessibility eliminates limited access to tools as an obstacle to design and construction.

The general awareness of the negative environmental impacts of plastic waste is effective in generating open-access movement towards implementing circularity in plastic waste management. This includes adapting industrial-scale plastic recycling processes to smaller scales to fit on a desktop. Recycling plastic waste, after washing, includes shredding plastic waste into small pieces and melting them down to produce filaments. These filaments can be used directly for filament extruders or pelletized for use with pellet extruders. This process is particularly suitable for plastic types that can be shredded and extruded without harming humans and the environment. Thereby, each small 3D printing workshop can have one desktop plastic reclaimer machine to shred failed 3D printed objects or plastic waste for extrusion. This helps to close the circle of plastic waste and enables the design of a closed-loop system that includes each process from manufacturing plastic objects to reusing plastic waste.

Applying a robotic industrial arm in 3D printings allows designers to design beyond the imposed dimension of a 3D printer's bed. This changes 3D printing from just prototyping towards printing building elements at a 1:1 scale. In the context of upcycling waste plastic, this will help architects manufacture building elements or architectural interior furniture. One approach is to use pellet extruders as a robot's end effectors to directly extrude shredded plastic waste. Thereby, there would be no need to produce filaments from shredded plastic waste. This simplification shortens the process of reclaiming plastic and reduces the printing time and energy.

Case Study: Layer-by-Layer Robotically 3D Printed Chair

One of the plastic types that is widely used in 3D printers at the UVA School of Architecture is Polylactic Acid (PLA). PLA is a biodegradable plastic that is considered Number 7 in the plastic waste categorization. Its biodegradation and low level of toxicity make it popular for prototyping architectural models. However, a huge amount of failed 3D printed prototypes is considered landfill waste, which justifies the development of a reclaiming process for this type of plastic. Establishing the reclaiming process can be extended to other non-toxic plastics such as Numbers 1 and 5.

Fig. D
The 3D printed chair in front of the robotic fabrication system.

Robotic Fused Deposition Modeling (FDM) is a layer-by-layer process of extruding polymers such as PLA. This layer-based process might differ from 3D printing with supports in that complex geometry is rationalized to have 3D printed supports for overhanging sections. Thereby, printing layers are designed to act as structural supports for upper layers. This manufacturing process reduces 3D printing time. Rationalizing complex geometries requires the integration of materials and fabrication constraints in design processes at the earliest stage of design.

This case study examined the robotic 3D printing of PLA to make a 1:1 scale chair. The aim was to test the formation to materialization stages to prepare this system to establish the circular plastic production of architectural furniture. An integrative computational tool was developed to assist with form generation. This tool integrates three main parameters involved in the production of a robotically 3D printed chair. These include PLA's mechanical and structural properties, limitations of the robotic fabrication system (KUKU KR120 R2700-2) and the pellet extruder head (MDPE10, Massive Dimension), and selected individual human parameters. Tilley (2002) in "The measure of man and woman" identified the human factors of designing ergonomic chairs (Tilley 2002). These design factors can be abstracted to user-based parameters to individualize each product, such as the height and width of the individual human body.

A series of experiments was conducted to identify the required parameters for 3D printing PLA palettes, such as the robot kinematic velocity, the temperature, and the revolutions per minute (RPM) of the extruder head. These experiments used a fixed 5mm nozzle to determine other parametric variables. The experiments included determining the inclination angles, width, and height of each 3D printed layer. These parameters shaped a parametric space as a design solution space for designing a chair.

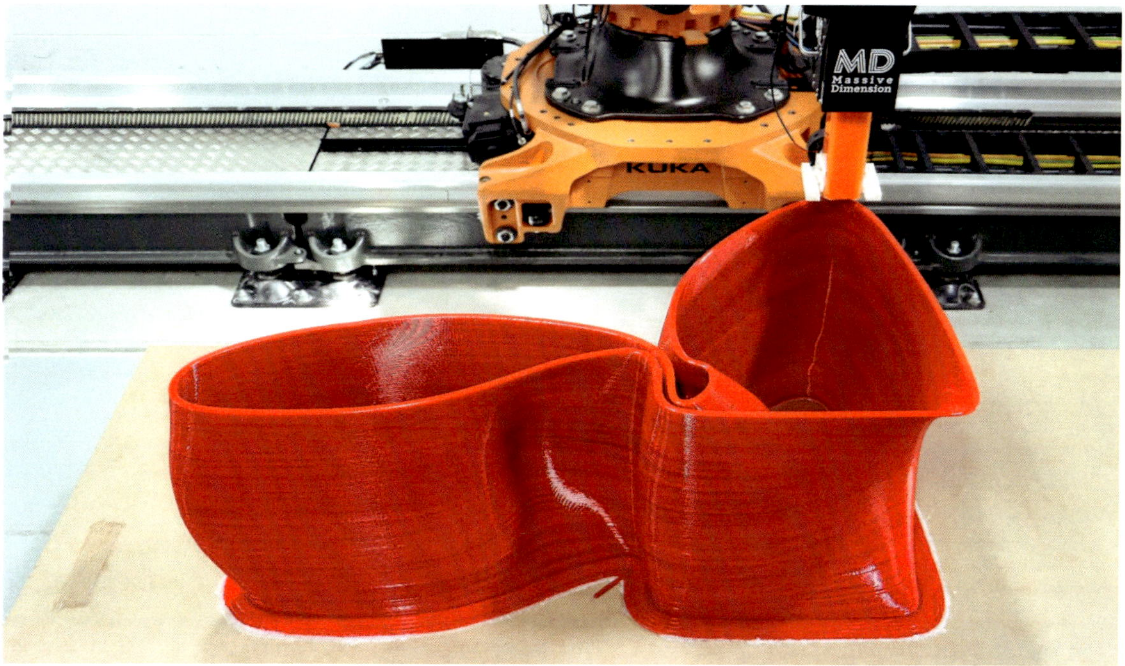

The result is an ergonomic chair, robotically 3D printed with PLA. In order to change the color of the chair, red color concentrates (3DXTECH) were added, which changed the translucency of the PLA to a spectrum of red color. The rate of red spectrum was calculated with the amount of red concentrate by weight to the overall weight of the pure PLA. The fully automated process of 3D printing includes the automatic feeding of pellets to the robotic fabrication system. A simple 3D printing bed was allocated for this purpose, which was calibrated for the robotic fabrication system. The overall process of robotically 3D printing this chair was between 14-16 hours, including everything from preparing the material to fully 3D printing the chair.

Discussion

This case study showcased the automation process of 3D printing an ergonomic chair, which is an everyday thing. The computational framework facilitates the integration of material properties and robotic fabrication systems, while parametrically allowing design adjustments to human parameters. The process of integrating material and fabrication parameters enables designers to exploit a design solution space curated with the specific material and fabrication system. This space, confined to the capacities and limitations of materialization processes, provides an exploratory space that monitors the constructability of the design. This encourages designers to embrace design agencies to address other needs of individuals. It provides a platform to consider human parameters as important factors of circular design. This computational interface allows designers to witness the process of formation located within their fabrication capacities.

Acknowledgements

I would like to thank student research assistants Avery Edson, Keaton Fisher, Juliana Jackson, Eli Sobel, and Tabi Summers for their invaluable assistance, as well as Melissa Goldman (Fabrication Lab Manager of the UVA School of Architecture) and Dr. Trevor Kemp (Fabrication Lab Assistant Manager of the UVA School of Architecture) for their profound support. In addition, I would like to thank the Jefferson Trust for funding this research project.

References:

Cheshire, David. *The Handbook to Building a Circular Economy.* Second edition. Newcastle upon Tyne: RIBA Publishing, 2021.

Faircloth, Billie. *Plastics Now: On Architecture's Relationship to a Continuously Emerging Material.* London, New York: Routledge Taylor & Francis Group, 2015.

Leonard, Annie and Ariane Conrad. *The Story of Stuff: How Our Obsession with Stuff Is Trashing the Planet, Our Communities, and Our Health— and a Vision for Change.* First Hardcover edition. New York: Free Press, 2010.

McDonough, William and Michael Braungart. *Cradle to Cradle: Remaking the Way We Make Things.* First edition. New York: North Point Press, 2002.

Meikle, Jeffrey L. *American Plastic: A Cultural History.* New Brunswick, NJ: Rutgers University Press, 1995.

Menges, Achim and Jan Knippers. *Architecture Research Building. ICD/ITKE 2010-2020.* Basel: Birkhäuser, 2021.

"National Overview: Facts and Figures on Materials, Wastes and Recycling." Environmental Protection Agency (EPA). Accessed November 22, 2023a. https://www.epa.gov/facts-and-figures-about-materials-waste-and-recycling/national-overview-facts-and-figures-materials.

"Plastics Product Manufacturing Waste Management Trend." Environmental Protection Agency (EPA). Accessed November 22, 2023b. https://www.epa.gov/trinationalanalysis/plastics-product-manufacturing-waste-management-trend.

Tilley, Alvin R. *The Measure of Man and Women: Human Factors in Design.* Revised edition. New York: Wiley, 2002.

"Towards the Circular Economy Vol. 1: An Economic and Business Rationale for an Accelerated Transition." Ellen MacArthur Foundation. 2013. https://www.ellenmacarthurfoundation.org/towards-the-circular-economy-vol-1-an-economic-and-business-rationale-for-an

"University of Virginia Sustainability 2020 – 2030 Plan." University of Virginia. 2022.

About the Author

Dr. Ehsan Baharlou is an Assistant Professor of Architecture at the University of Virginia School of Architecture. His work focuses on ecological construction to meet the challenges of climate change through research on sustainable materials and robotic construction. He explores novel design strategies to shift the design approach from material- and fabrication-centered design processes to multispecies design.

Dr. Baharlou's research projects focus on utilizing additive manufacturing techniques to explore the emergence of computational tectonics through materiality. His research projects on the development of bioprinting involve using mycelium to engineer living materials for biomanufacturing. They also include developing innovative methods to embed greenery within 3D printed soil, especially in a way that integrates biomaterial with design and fabrication. In addition, he investigates techniques to upcycle waste materials, such as waste plastic, and the role that this might play in the future of construction.

His previous projects include developing a mobile robotic system for in situ additive manufacturing with soil-based material, devising a novel hybrid composite system, exploring possibilities in the robotic assembly of timber structures, and investigating adaptive additive manufacturing techniques.

Dr. Baharlou completed his postdoctoral associate in 2018 at the Massachusetts Institute of Technology, where he focused on the automated production of composite architecture. He earned his doctoral degree (Dr.-Ing.) in 2017 under the supervision of Professor Achim Menges at the Institute for Computational Design and Construction (ICD) at the University of Stuttgart. Dr. Baharlou's doctoral research focused on the integration of fabrication and construction constraints into a computational model for the realization of informed form generation. His earlier teaching experiences include leading several international workshops on computational design and robotic fabrication, and teaching undergraduate and graduate students at ICD.

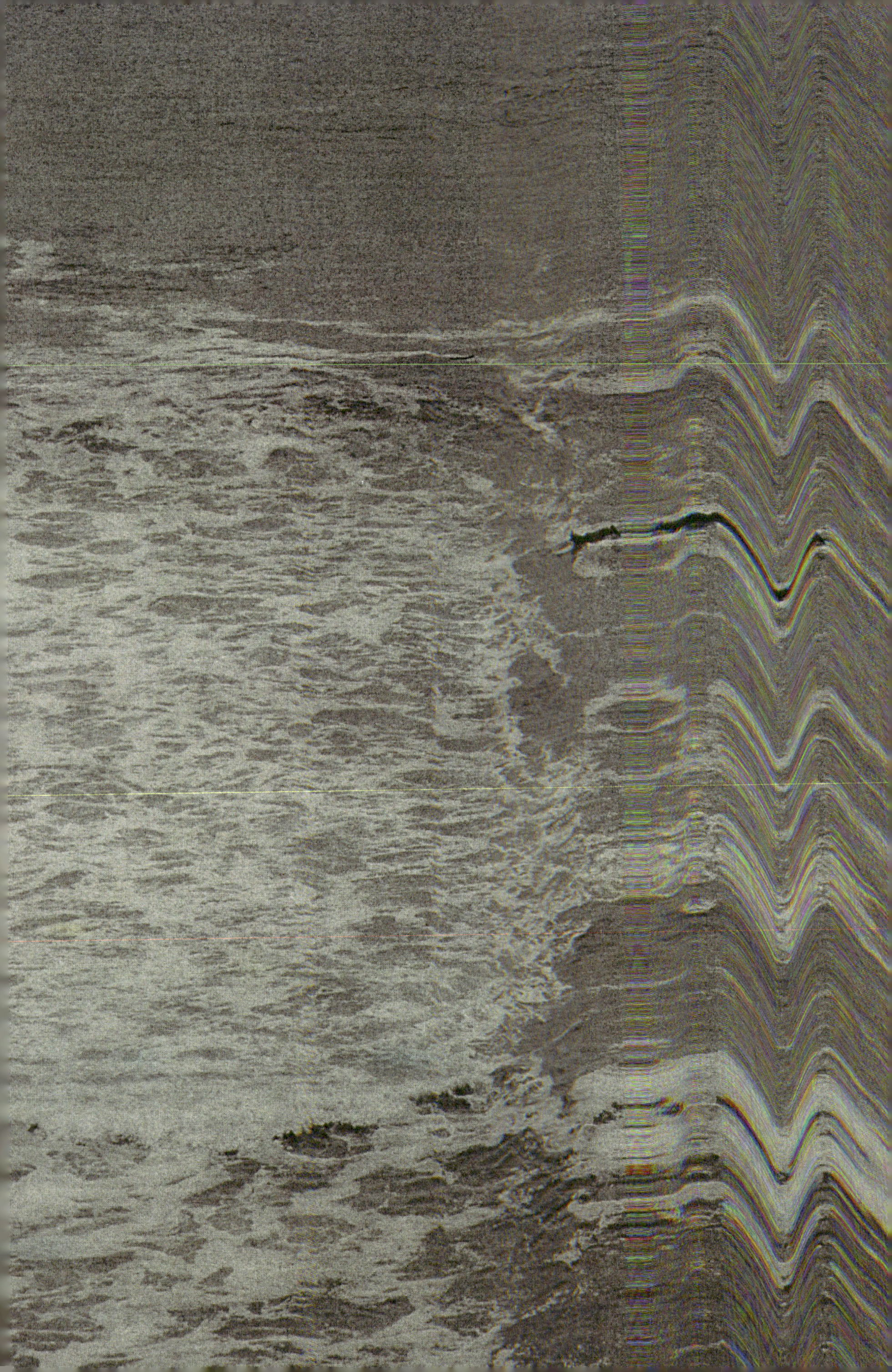

Ariana Arenius
JT Bachman
Ehsan Baharlou
Shirley (Dongwei) Chen
Judy Shao-Yu Chen
Amanda Coen
Isaac Cohen
Alex Daley
Phillip Edmonston
Clara Gardner
Lara Call Gastinger
Sean Kois
Zhouhan Li
Ryan Moody
Paul Mosley
Zlata Onufrieva
François Penz
Emma Potter
Patrick Sardo
Eli Sobel
Katie Stranix
Emily Wettstein

Contributing Authors

APPLIED
RESEARCH
+DESIGN